Praise for ...

CRAZY LOVE

"Chan writes with infectious exuberance, challenging Christians to take the Bible seriously. The book offers real-life accounts of believers who have given all—time, money, health, even their lives—in obedience to Christ's call. Earnest Christians will find valuable take-home lessons from Chan's excellent book."

Publishers Weekly

"In Francis Chan's unique style, and with an urgency that seeks to awaken a sleeping church mired in the comfort of middle ground, *Crazy Love* quickly gets to the heart of the matter and leaves you wanting more ... more of the matchless Jesus who offers radical life for all right now."

Louie Giglio, visionary architect, director
of Passion Conferences, and author
of *I Am Not, but I Know I AM*

"Francis's life reflects authentic leadership tempered by a deep compassion for the lost, the last, the littlest, and the least. In his fresh new book, *Crazy Love*, Francis peels back what we think the Christian life is, and guides us down the path toward an uncommon intimacy with Jesus—an intimacy which can't help but change the world around us!"

Joni Eareckson Tada, best-
selling author and speaker

"In an age of religious phonies, spiritual apathy, and disheartening books suggesting that God is a delusion, *Crazy Love* shines like a glorious beacon of hope and light. Francis Chan effuses love for Jesus Christ and demonstrates practical ways to throw off lukewarm Christianity and embrace full-on, passionate love for God."

Kirk Cameron, actor and author of *Still Growing*

Praise for …

FORGOTTEN GOD

"Are you spiritually empty and searching for something more? Francis Chan imparts a life-changing message on the power of the Holy Spirit and His desire to unleash Himself into our daily lives."

Craig Groeschel, founding pastor of
LifeChurch.tv and author of *It: How Churches
and Leaders Can Get It and Keep It*

"No church and no Christian can be healthy or attain maturity without a life lived in and led by the Spirit. Francis Chan's latest book is a timely reminder and engaging encouragement to get intimately acquainted with the Forgotten God."

Simon Ponsonby, Bible teacher,
pastor, and author of *And the Lamb
Wins, More*, and *God Inside Out*

crazy love

OVERWHELMED
BY A RELENTLESS
GOD

FRANCIS CHAN | **2-IN-1**

with danae yankoski

FORGOTTEN GOD
REVERSING OUR TRAGIC NEGLECT OF THE HOLY SPIRIT

David C Cook®
transforming lives together

CRAZY LOVE/FORGOTTEN GOD 2-IN-1
Published by David C Cook
4050 Lee Vance View
Colorado Springs, CO 80918 U.S.A.

David C Cook Distribution Canada
55 Woodslee Avenue, Paris, Ontario, Canada N3L 3E5

David C Cook U.K., Kingsway Communications
Eastbourne, East Sussex BN23 6NT, England

The graphic circle C logo is a registered trademark of David C Cook.
The *Crazy Love* title treatment with arrows is a registered trademark of David C Cook.

ISBN 978-1-4347-0886-1

© 2014 Francis Chan
Published in association with the literary agency of D. C. Jacobson
& Associates LLC, an Author Management Company
www.dcjacobson.com.

The Team: Ingrid Beck, Nick Lee, Amy Konyndyk, and Karen Athen
Cover Design: Nick Lee
Author Photo: Daley Hake

Printed in the United States of America
First Edition 2014

1 2 3 4 5 6 7 8 9 10

052814

CRAZY LOVE
LCCN 2008922793
ISBN 978-1-4347-0594-5
eISBN 978-0-7814-1103-5
© 2013 Francis Chan
Published in association with the literary agency of D. C. Jacobson & Associates LLC,
an Author Management Company www.dcjacobson.com.
First edition published by David C Cook in 2008 ©
Francis Chan, ISBN 978-1-4347-6851-3.
Cover Design: Jim Elliston

FORGOTTEN GOD
LCCN 2009929661
ISBN 978-1-4347-6795-0
eISBN 978-0-7814-0350-4
© 2009 Francis Chan
Published in association with the literary agency of
D.C. Jacobson & Associates LLC, an Author Management Company
www.DCJacobson.com
Cover Design: The Regime, Jim Elliston

↓↑

crazy love

OVERWHELMED
BY A RELENTLESS
GOD

FRANCIS CHAN
with danae yankoski

Heavenly Father, thank You for Your grace. Your forgiveness is SO good that I struggle with believing it at times. Thank You for rescuing me from myself and giving me Your Holy Spirit. Your love is better than life.

To my best friend, Lisa,
for being a godly, gorgeous, excellent wife and mother

ACKNOWLEDGMENTS

Thanks to …

Danae Yankoski for all of the effort and heart you put into this book.

Don and Jenni at DC Jacobson and Associates for your encouragement
and help.

Todd and Joshua for serving the church and college God has given us
to lead.

My assistant, Sandy, for being a great helper and a cool old lady.

The members of Cornerstone Church for passionately pursuing God
with me.

CONTENTS

FOREWORD

It is with great excitement and honor that I get the opportunity to introduce you to my friend Francis Chan. Francis is one of those rare people you come across in life who leaves you wanting to be better. You know, a better friend, a better neighbor, a better athlete (well maybe not athlete … I can take Francis in most things involving competition). But most important, Francis leaves you wanting more of Jesus. If you are around Francis for more than thirty minutes, you soon realize that he is a man with great vision and resolve for the mission of Jesus. Some might say that Francis is a bit of an idealist in thinking that one life can really make a dent in the world. But I would say that Francis is the ultimate realist. Meaning, someone who believes that God is really who He says He is and that the true reality of this life is to follow Him wholeheartedly.

The book you have in your hand, *Crazy Love*, may just be the most challenging book outside of God's Word you will read this year. (And for a few years to come for that matter.) The status quo and norms of the so-called "Christian" life that so many of us are used to experiencing are in for a shock! Isn't it interesting that in Acts 11, at the end of verse 26, it says, "The disciples were called Christians first at Antioch." What I find interesting is the simple thought that the Christians didn't name themselves. But rather, they were *called* (or named) "Christians" by those watching their lives. I wonder if it would be the same today. Could someone look at your life or look at my life and name me a Christian? A humbling question for sure.

Crazy Love is the perfect title for this book. When Jesus was asked, "What is the greatest commandment?" he responded with "Love."

> "Love the Lord your God with all your heart and with all your soul and with all your mind." This is the first and greatest commandment. And the second is like it: "Love your neighbor as yourself." (Matt. 22:37–40)

As Francis so brilliantly illustrates, the life that Jesus calls us to is absolute craziness to the world. Sure, it's fine and politically correct to *believe* in God, but to really *love* Him is a whole different story. Yeah, it's nice and generous to give to the needy at Christmas or after some disaster, but to sacrifice your own comfort and welfare for another may look like madness to a safe and undisturbed world.

I am challenged to the core by the pages you're about to read. I am excited that you are diving into this much-needed book. I encourage you to face up to the convictions of *Crazy Love*. I know your heart and spirit will be stirred again for your First Love.

—Chris Tomlin,
songwriter and worship leader of Passion Conferences

Discover More Online:

Watch Francis introduce each chapter at www.CrazyLoveBook.com.

 Introduction Chapter 1 Chapter 2

PREFACE TO THE UPDATED EDITION

I write this preface in January of 2013, and as of now *Crazy Love* has sold more than two million copies. To say that the response to the book surprised me is a huge understatement.

When I wrote *Crazy Love*, I assumed I was only appealing to a small segment of the population. I hoped to encourage those who were confused by the church system—those who had been made to feel crazy because of their desire to follow Scripture simply and literally. I had no idea that it would resonate with so many people.

I have seen some positive developments in the American church since 2008. I see a greater awareness of the suffering of those in our hometowns and those around the world. More people now question what it really means to "follow Jesus" and actively evaluate their lifestyles. Some have recognized their need to surrender and have repented of their ways. And in those individuals and churches that are pursuing these things, I see more joy and vitality.

I love the church, and I am encouraged as I travel around the country and around the world and see groups of people living as God intended His church to live. I see the Spirit working—*as He always is*—and I am encouraged to see a larger group within the American church taking Scripture seriously and following the Spirit's leading.

But this is no reason to settle in. We will always find ourselves in trouble when we get comfortable with things as they are.

As I reflect on what I wrote here five years ago, there are some things that would probably come out a bit differently if I were writing them today. Some have said that I focused too much on needs overseas and didn't focus enough on the person who is called to the workplace here in America. I didn't emphasize the need to work hard at our jobs to the glory of God. Everything I wrote in *Crazy Love*—seeing God accurately, loving Him passionately, taking the Scriptures at face value, etc.—needs to be applied in every area of our lives.

Crazy Love will never be the only message the church needs to hear, but I am thankful that it continues to speak to people. Five years later, we still need to be reminded that God is bigger than we think. We need to be awed by His unfathomable love for us. We need to be pushed away from the lukewarm equilibrium we keep coming back to. I still need these reminders, and the church does too.

In this edition of *Crazy Love*, I have added an additional chapter to update readers on my ministry and my thought process. God continues to guide and teach me, and I wanted to share some of that. Aside from that additional chapter, the text remains almost identical to the 2008 edition. This means that there is a five-year gap between chapters 1–10 and chapter 11. I decided not to change the references in those original chapters to where I was living, how many children I had, and where and how I was ministering. I wanted to change those chapters as little as possible since people have been connecting with them so well over the years.

As you read this new edition of *Crazy Love*, my prayer for you is the same as it was when I first wrote it. I want you to be challenged by God's greatness and love. I want you to understand that the only sane response to His love is a wholehearted devotion to Jesus. And I want you to see that the crazy people in this world are those who experience God's love and remain complacent, not those who let go of all they have and follow Him completely.

PREFACE

To just read the Bible, attend church, and avoid "big" sins—
is this passionate, wholehearted love for God?
—François Fénelon, *The Seeking Heart*

We all know something's wrong.

At first I thought it was just me. Then I stood before twenty thousand Christian college students and asked, "How many of you have read the New Testament and wondered if we in the church are missing it?" When almost every hand went up, I felt comforted. At least I'm not crazy.

In this book I am going to ask some hard questions. They will resonate with what a lot of us feel but are generally afraid to articulate and explore. Don't worry—this isn't another book written to bash churches. I think it's far too easy to blame the American church without acknowledging that we are each part of the church and therefore responsible. But I think we all feel deeply, even if we haven't voiced it, that the church in many ways is not doing well.

I get nervous when I think of how we've missed who we are supposed to be, and sad when I think about how we're missing out on all that God wants for the people He loved enough to die for.

I haven't always felt this way. I grew up believing in God without having a clue what He is like. I called myself a Christian, was pretty involved in church, and tried to stay away from all of the things that "good Christians" avoid—drinking, drugs, sex, swearing. Christianity was simple: Fight your desires in order to please God. Whenever I failed (which was often), I'd walk around feeling guilty and distant from God.

In hindsight, I don't think my church's teachings were incorrect, just incomplete. My view of God was narrow and small.

Now I am a husband, a father of four, and the pastor of a church in Southern California. Until just a few years ago I was quite happy with how God was working in me and in the church. Then God began changing my heart. This took place largely during the times I spent reading His Word. The conviction I felt through the teachings of Scripture, coupled with several experiences in third-world countries, changed everything. Some serious paradigm shattering happened in my life, and consequently in our church.

The result is that I've never felt more alive, and neither has Cornerstone Church. It's exhilarating to be part of a group of believers who are willing to think biblically rather than conventionally, to be part of a body where radical living is becoming the norm.

This book is written for those who want more Jesus. It is for those who are bored with what American Christianity offers. It is for those who don't want to plateau, those who would rather die before their convictions do.

I hope reading this book will convince you of something: that by surrendering yourself totally to God's purposes, He will bring you the most pleasure in this life and the next. I hope it affirms your desire for "more God"—even if you are surrounded by people who feel they have "enough God." I hope it inspires confidence if you have questioned and doubted the commitment of the American church. I want to affirm your questioning, even while assuring you there is hope.

God put me in Simi Valley, California, to lead a church of comfortable people into lives of risk and adventure. I believe He wants us to love others so much that we go to extremes to help them. I believe He wants us to be known for giving—of our time, our money, and our abilities—and to start a movement of "giving" churches. In so doing, we can alleviate the suffering in the world and change the reputation of His bride in America. Some people, even some at my church, have told me flat-out, "You're crazy." But I can't imagine devoting my life to a greater vision.

We need to stop giving people excuses not to believe in God. You've probably heard the expression "I believe in God, just not organized religion." I don't think people would say that if the church truly lived like we are called to live. The expression would change to "I can't deny what the church does, but I don't believe in their God." At least then they'd address their rejection of God rather than use the church as a scapegoat.

We are going to look at how the Bible calls us to live our lives. It is important that we not measure our spiritual health by the people around us, who are pretty much like us. To begin this journey, we'll first address our inaccurate view of God and, consequently, of ourselves.

But before we look at what is wrong and address it, we need to understand something. The core problem isn't the fact that we're lukewarm, halfhearted, or stagnant Christians. The crux of it all is why we are this way, and it is because we have an inaccurate view of God. We see Him as a benevolent Being who is satisfied when people manage to fit Him into their lives in some small way. We forget that God never had an identity crisis. He knows that He's great and deserves to be the center of our lives. Jesus came humbly as a servant, but He never begs us to give Him some small part of ourselves. He commands everything from His followers.

The first three chapters are absolutely foundational to this book. Though parts of it may not be "new" material to you, allow these sacred truths to move you to worship. I pray that your reading of the next few pages will be interrupted by spontaneous and meaningful praise to God. Allow these words to communicate old truths to your heart in a fresh way.

After the foundation has been laid in the first three chapters, the last seven chapters call us to examine ourselves. We will address life in light of the crux of who God is. We'll discover what is wrong in our churches and, ultimately, in ourselves.

Come with me on this journey. I don't promise it will be pain-less. Change, as we all know, is uncomfortable. It's up to you to respond to what you read. But you will have a choice: to adjust how you live daily or to stay the same.

stop praying

What if I said, *"Stop praying"*? What if I told you to stop talking *at* God for a while, but instead to take a long, hard look at Him before you speak another word? Solomon warned us not to rush into God's presence with words. That's what fools do. And often, that's what we do.

We are a culture that relies on technology over community, a society in which spoken and written words are cheap, easy to come by, and excessive. Our culture says anything goes; fear of God is almost unheard of. We are slow to listen, quick to speak, and quick to become angry.

The wise man comes to God without saying a word and stands in awe of Him. It may seem a hopeless endeavor, to gaze at the invisible God. But Romans 1:20 tells us that through creation, we see His "invisible qualities" and "divine nature."

Let's begin this book by gazing at God in silence. What I want you to do right now is to go online and look at the "Awe Factor" video at www.crazylovebook.com to get a taste of the awe factor of our God. Seriously—go do it.

Speechless? Amazed? Humbled?

When I first saw those images, I *had* to worship. I didn't want to speak to or share it with anyone. I just wanted to sit quietly and admire the Creator.

It's wild to think that most of these galaxies have been discovered only in the past few years, thanks to the Hubble telescope. They've been in the universe for thousands of years without humans even knowing about them.

Why would God create more than 350,000,000,000 galaxies (and this is a conservative estimate) that generations of people never saw or even knew existed? Do you think maybe it was to make us say, "Wow, God is unfathomably big"? Or perhaps God wanted us to see these pictures so that our response would be, "Who do I think I am?"

R. C. Sproul writes, "Men are never duly touched and impressed with a conviction of their insignificance, until they have contrasted themselves with the majesty of God."[1]

Switch gears with me for a minute and think about the detailed intricacy of the other side of creation.

Did you know that a caterpillar has 228 separate and distinct muscles in its head? That's quite a few, for a bug. The average elm tree has approximately *6 million* leaves on it. And your own heart generates enough pressure as it pumps blood throughout your body that it could squirt blood up to 30 feet. (I've never tried this, and I don't recommend it.)

Have you ever thought about how diverse and creative God is? He didn't have to make hundreds of different kinds of bananas, but He did. He didn't have to put 3,000 different species of trees within one square mile in the Amazon jungle, but He did. God didn't have to create so many kinds of laughter. Think about the different sounds of your friends' laughs—wheezes, snorts, silent, loud, obnoxious.

How about the way plants defy gravity by drawing water upward from the ground into their stems and veins? Or did you know that spiders produce three kinds of silk? When they build their webs, they create sixty feet of silk in one hour, simultaneously producing special oil on their feet that prevents them from sticking to their own web. (Most of us hate spiders, but sixty feet an hour deserves some respect!) Coral plants are so sensitive that they can die if the water temperature varies by even one or two degrees.

Did you know that when you get goose bumps, the hair in your follicles is actually helping you stay warmer by trapping body heat? Or what about the simple fact that plants take in carbon dioxide (which is harmful to us) and produce oxygen (which we need to survive)? I'm sure you knew that, but have you ever marveled at it? And these same poison-swallowing, life-giving plants came from tiny seeds that were placed in the dirt. Some were watered, some weren't;

but after a few days they poked through the soil and out into the warm sunlight.

Whatever God's reasons for such diversity, creativity, and sophistication in the universe, on earth, and in our own bodies, the point of it all is His glory. God's art speaks of Himself, reflecting who He is and what He is like.

> The heavens declare the glory of God; the skies proclaim the work of his hands. Day after day they pour forth speech; night after night they display knowledge. There is no speech or language where their voice is not heard. Their voice goes out into all the earth, their words to the ends of the world.
>
> —Psalm 19:1–4

This is why we are called to worship Him. His art, His handiwork, and His creation all echo the truth that He is glorious. There is no other like Him. He is the King of Kings, the Beginning and the End, the One who was and is and is to come. I know you've heard this before, but I don't want you to miss it.

I sometimes struggle with how to properly respond to God's magnitude in a world bent on ignoring or merely tolerating Him. But know this: God will not be tolerated. He instructs us to worship and fear Him.

Go back and reread the last two paragraphs. Go to the website www.crazylovebook.com and watch the "Just Stop and Think" fifteen-minute video. Close this book if you need to, and meditate on the almighty One who dwells in unapproachable light, the glorious One.

↓↑

There is an epidemic of spiritual amnesia going around, and none of us is immune. No matter how many fascinating details we learn about God's creation, no matter how many pictures we see of His galaxies, and no matter how many sunsets we watch, we still forget.

Most of us know that we are supposed to love and fear God; that we are supposed to read our Bibles and pray so that we can get to know Him better; that we are supposed to worship Him with our lives. But actually living it out is challenging.

It confuses us when loving God is hard. Shouldn't it be easy to love a God so wonderful? When we love God because we feel we *should* love Him, instead of genuinely loving out of our true selves, we have forgotten who God really is. Our amnesia is flaring up again.

It may sound "un-Christian" to say that on some mornings I don't feel like loving God, or I just forget to. But I do. In our world, where hundreds of things distract us from God, we have to intentionally and consistently remind ourselves of Him.

I recently attended my high school reunion. People kept coming up to me and saying, "She's *your* wife?" They were amazed, I guess, that a woman so beautiful would marry someone like me. It happened enough times that I took a good look at a photograph of the two of us. I, too, was taken aback. It *is* astonishing that my wife chooses to be with me—and not just because she is beautiful. I was reminded of the fullness of what I have been given in my wife.

We need the same sort of reminders about God's goodness. We are programmed to focus on what we don't have, bombarded multiple times throughout the day with what we need to buy that will make us feel happier or sexier or more at peace. This dissatisfaction transfers over to our thinking about God. We forget that we already have everything we need in Him. Because we don't often think about the reality of who God is, we quickly forget that He is worthy to be worshipped and loved. We are to fear Him.

A. W. Tozer writes,

> What comes into our minds when we think about God is the most important thing about us.... Worship is pure or base as the worshiper entertains high or low thoughts of God. For this reason the gravest question before the Church is always God Himself, and the most portentous fact about any man is not what he at a given time may say or do, but what he in his deep heart conceives God to be like.[2]

If the "gravest question" before us really is what God Himself is like, how do we learn to know Him?

We have seen how He is the Creator of both the magnitude of the galaxies and the complexity of caterpillars. But what is He like? What are His characteristics? What are His defining attributes? How are we to fear Him? To speak to Him? Don't check out here. We need to be reminded of this stuff. It is both basic and crucial.

God is holy. A lot of people say that whatever you believe about God is fine, so long as you are sincere. But that is comparable to describing your friend in one instance as a three-hundred-pound sumo wrestler and in another as a five-foot-two, ninety-pound gymnast. No matter how sincere you are in your explanations, both descriptions of your friend simply cannot be true.

The preposterous part about our doing this to God is that He already has a name, an identity. We don't get to decide who God is. "God said to Moses, 'I AM WHO I AM'" (Ex. 3:14). We don't change that.

To say that God is holy is to say that He is set apart, distinct from us. And because of His set apart-ness, there is no way we can ever fathom all of who He is. To the Jews, saying something three times demonstrated its perfection, so to call God "Holy, Holy, Holy" is to say that He is perfectly set apart, with nothing and no one to compare Him to. *That* is what it means to be "holy."

Many Spirit-filled authors have exhausted the thesaurus in order to describe God with the glory He deserves. His perfect holiness, by definition, assures us that our words can't contain Him. Isn't it a comfort to worship a God we cannot exaggerate?

God is eternal. Most of us would probably agree with that statement. But have you ever seriously meditated on what it means? Each of us had a beginning; everything in existence began on a particular day, at a specific time.

Everything, that is, but God. He always has been, since before there was an earth, a universe, or even angels. God exists outside of time, and since we are within time, there is no way we will ever totally grasp that concept.

Not being able to fully understand God is frustrating, but it is ridiculous for us to think we have the right to limit God to something we are capable of comprehending. What a stunted, insignificant god *that* would be! If my mind is the size of a soda can and God is the size of all the oceans, it would be stupid for me to say He is only the small amount of water I can scoop into my little can. God is so much bigger, so far beyond our time-encased, air/food/sleep–dependent lives.

Please stop here, even if just for a moment, and glorify the eternal God: "But you, O Lord, sit enthroned forever; your renown endures through all generations.... But you remain the same, and your years will never end" (Ps. 102:12, 27).

God is all-knowing. Isn't this an intimidating thought?

Each of us, to some degree, fools our friends and family about who we really are. But it's impossible to do that with God. He knows each of us, deeply and specifically. He knows our thoughts before we think them, our actions before we commit them, whether we are lying down or sitting or walking around. He knows who we are and what we are about. We cannot escape Him, not even if we want to. When I grow weary of trying to be faithful to Him and want a break, it doesn't come as a surprise to God.

For David, God's knowledge led him to worship. He viewed it as wonderful and meaningful. He wrote in Psalm 139 that even in the darkness he couldn't hide from God; that while he was in his mother's womb, God was there.

Hebrews 4:13 says, "Nothing in all creation is hidden from God's sight. Everything is uncovered and laid bare before the eyes of him to whom we must give account." It is sobering to realize that this is the same God who is holy and eternal, the Maker of the billions of galaxies and thousands of tree species in the rainforest. This is the God who takes the time to know all the little details about each of us. He does not have to know us so well, but He chooses to.

God is all-powerful. Colossians 1:16 tells us that everything was created *for* God: "For by him all things were created: things in heaven and on earth, visible and invisible, whether thrones or powers or rulers or authorities; all things were created by him and for him."

Don't we live instead as though God is created for *us*, to do *our* bidding, to bless *us*, and to take care of *our* loved ones?

Psalm 115:3 reveals, "Our God is in heaven; he does whatever pleases him." Yet we keep on questioning Him: "Why did You make me with this body, instead of that one?" "Why are so many people dying of starvation?" "Why are there so many planets with nothing living on them?" "Why is my family so messed up?" "Why don't You make Yourself more obvious to the people who need You?"

The answer to each of these questions is simply this: because He's God. He has more of a right to ask us why so many people are starving. As much as we want God to explain Himself to us, His creation, we are in no place to demand that He give an account to us.

> All the peoples of the earth are regarded as nothing.
> He does as he pleases with the powers of heaven and
> the peoples of the earth. No one can hold back his
> hand or say to him: "What have you done?"
> —Daniel 4:35

Can you worship a God who isn't obligated to explain His actions to you? Could it be your arrogance that makes you think God owes you an explanation?

Do you really believe that compared to God, "all the peoples of the earth are regarded as nothing," including you?

God is fair and just. One definition of justice is "reward and/or penalty as deserved." If what we truly deserved were up to us, we would end up with as many different answers as people who responded. But it isn't up to us, mostly because none of us are good.

God is the only Being who is good, and the standards are set by Him. Because God hates sin, He has to punish those guilty of sin. Maybe that's not an appealing standard. But to put it bluntly, when you get your own universe, you can make your own standards. When we disagree, let's not assume it's His reasoning that needs correction.

It takes a lot for us to comprehend God's total hatred for sin. We make excuses like, "Yes, I am prideful at times, but everyone struggles with pride." However, God says in Proverbs 8:13, "I *hate* pride and arrogance." You and I are not allowed to tell Him how much He can hate it. He can hate and punish it as severely as His justice demands.

God never excuses sin. And He is always consistent with that ethic. Whenever we start to question whether God really hates sin, we have only to think of the cross, where His Son was tortured, mocked, and beaten because of sin. *Our* sin.

No question about it: God hates and must punish sin. And He is totally just and fair in doing so.

Before the Throne

So far we have talked about things we can see with our own eyes, things we know about creation, and some of the attributes of God as revealed in the Bible. But many facets of God expand beyond our comprehension. He cannot be contained in this world, explained by our vocabulary, or grasped by our understanding.

Yet in Revelation 4 and Isaiah 6 we get two distinct glimpses of the heavenly throne room. Let me paint a bit of a word picture for you.

In Revelation, when John recounts his experience of seeing God, it's as though he's scrambling for earthly words to describe the vision he was privileged to see. He describes the One seated on the throne with two gems, "jasper and carnelian," and the area around the throne as a rainbow that looked like an emerald. God, the One on the throne, resembles radiant jewels more than flesh and blood.

This sort of poetic, artistic imagery can be difficult for those of us who don't think that way. So imagine the most stunning sunset you've ever seen. Remember the radiant colors splashed across the sky? The way you stopped to gaze at it in awe? And how the words *wow* and *beautiful* seemed so lacking? That's a small bit of what John is talking about in Revelation 4 as he attempts to articulate his vision of heaven's throne room.

John describes "flashes of lightning" and "rumblings and peals of thunder" coming from God's throne, a throne that must be unlike any other. He writes that before the throne are seven blazing torches and something like a sea of glass that looks like crystal. Using ordinary words, he does his best to describe a heavenly place and a holy God.

Most intriguing to me is how John describes those who surround the throne. First, there are the twenty-four elders dressed in white and wearing golden crowns. Next, John describes four six-winged beings with eyes all over their bodies and wings. One has the face of a lion, one of an ox, one of a man, and one of an eagle.

I try to imagine what it would be like if I actually saw one of these creatures out in the woods or down at the beach. I would probably pass out! It would be terrifying to see a being with the face of a lion and eyes "all around and within."

As if John's description isn't wild and strange enough, he then tells us what the beings are saying. The twenty-four elders cast their gold crowns before the One on the throne, fall on their faces before Him, and say, "You are worthy, our Lord and God, to receive glory and honor and power, for you created all things, and by your will they were created and have their being." At the same time, the four creatures never stop (day or night) saying, "Holy, holy, holy is the Lord God Almighty, who was, and is, and is to come!" Just imagine being in that room, surrounded by the elders chanting God's worth, and the creatures declaring God's holiness.

The prophet Isaiah also had a vision of God in His throne room, but this time it is a more direct picture: "I saw the Lord seated on a throne."

Wow. Isaiah saw that and lived? The Israelites hid themselves whenever God passed by their camp because they were too afraid to look at Him, even the back of Him as He moved away. They were scared they would die if they saw God.

But Isaiah looked and saw God. He writes that the bottom of God's robe filled the whole temple, and that the seraphim appeared above Him. The seraphim each had six wings, similar to the creatures John describes in Revelation. Isaiah says they called out to one another, saying, "Holy, holy, holy is the Lord Almighty; the whole earth is full of his glory!" Then the foundations shook and smoke filled the house, which is similar to John's description of flashes of lightning and peals of thunder.

Isaiah's description is less detailed than John's, but Isaiah shares more of his response to being in the throne room of God. His words reverberate in the wake of the smoky room and shaky foundation: "Woe is me.... I am ruined! For I am a man of unclean lips, and my eyes have seen the King, the Lord Almighty." And then one of the seraphim brings Isaiah a piece of burning coal that had been smoldering on the altar. The creature touches Isaiah's mouth with the hot coal and tells him that his guilt is taken away.

Both of these descriptions serve a purpose. John's helps us imagine what the throne room of God looks like, while Isaiah's reminds us what our only response to such a God should be.

May Isaiah's cry become our own. Woe is me ... we are a people of unclean lips!

Perhaps you need to take a deep breath after thinking about the God who made galaxies and caterpillars, the One who sits enthroned and eternally praised by beings so fascinating that were they photographed, it would make prime-time news for weeks. If you are not staggered, go to Isaiah 6 and Revelation 4 and read the accounts aloud and slowly, doing your best to imagine what the authors describe.

The appropriate way to end this chapter is the same way we began it—by standing in awed silence before a mighty, fearsome God, whose tremendous worth becomes even more apparent as we see our own puny selves in comparison.

you might not finish this chapter

You could die before you finish reading this chapter. I could die while you're reading it. Today. At any moment.

But it's easy to think about today as just another day. An average day where you go about life concerned with your to-do list, preoccupied by appointments, focused on family, thinking about your desires and needs.

On the average day, we live caught up in ourselves. On the average day, we don't consider God very much. On the average day, we forget that our life truly is a vapor.

But there is nothing normal about today. Just think about everything that must function properly just for you to survive. For example, your kidneys. The only people who really think about their kidneys are people whose kidneys don't work correctly. The majority of us take for granted our kidneys, liver, lungs, and other internal organs that we're dependent upon to continue living.

What about driving down the road at sixty-five miles per hour, only a few feet away from cars going the opposite direction at the same speed? Someone would only have to jerk his or her arm and you would be dead. I don't think that's morbid; I think it's reality.

It's crazy that we think today is just a normal day to do whatever we want with. To those of us who say, "Today or tomorrow we will go to this or that city, spend a year there, carry on business and make money," James writes, "Why, you do not even know what will happen tomorrow. What is your life? You are a mist that appears for a little while and then vanishes" (4:13–14).

When you think about it, that's a little disconcerting. But even after reading those verses, do you really believe you could vanish at any minute? That perhaps today you will die? Or do you instead feel somehow invincible?

Frederick Buechner writes, "Intellectually we all know that we will die, but we do not really know it in the sense that the knowledge becomes a part of us. We do not really know it in the sense of living as though it were true. On the contrary, we tend to live as though our lives would go on forever."[3]

Justified Stress?

I had never experienced heart problems until a couple of years ago when I began to have heart palpitations. Over time they became more frequent, and this worried me.

I finally told my wife. In case something happened to me, I didn't want it to come as a complete shock. She suggested I go to the doctor, but I resisted because I'm stubborn and that's what I do.

You see, when I was honest I knew what the problem was. I was immersed in and overcome by stress. It was the Christmas season, and I had to take care of and think about a lot of things.

But on Christmas Eve the issue intensified so much that I told my wife I would go to the emergency room after the church service. During the service, however, I surrendered all of my worries and stress to God. My symptoms slowly went away, and I never went to the doctor.

I used to believe that in this world there are two kinds of people: natural worriers and naturally joyful people. I couldn't really help it that I was the worrying kind. I'm a problem solver, so I have to focus on things that need fixing. God can see that my intensity and anxiety are ministry related. I worry because I take His work seriously.

Right?

But then there's that perplexing command: "*Rejoice in the Lord always.* I will say it again: Rejoice!" (Phil. 4:4). You'll notice that it doesn't end with "... unless you're doing something extremely important." No, it's a command for all of us, and it follows with the charge, "Do not be anxious about anything" (v. 6).

That came as a pretty staggering realization. But what I realized next was even more staggering.

When I am consumed by my problems—stressed out about *my* life, *my* family, and *my* job—I actually convey the belief that I think the circumstances are more important than God's command to always rejoice. In other words, that I have a "right" to disobey God because of the magnitude of my responsibilities.

Worry implies that we don't quite trust that God is big enough, powerful enough, or loving enough to take care of what's happening in our lives.

Stress says that the things we are involved in are important enough to merit our impatience, our lack of grace toward others, or our tight grip of control.

Basically, these two behaviors communicate that it's okay to sin and not trust God because the stuff in my life is somehow exceptional. Both worry and stress reek of arrogance. They declare our tendency to forget that we've been forgiven, that our lives here are brief, that we are headed to a place where we won't be lonely, afraid, or hurt ever again, and that in the context of God's strength, our problems are small, indeed.

Why are we so quick to forget God? Who do we think we are?

I find myself relearning this lesson often. Even though I glimpse God's holiness, I am still dumb enough to forget that life is all about God and not about me at all.

It goes sort of like this....

Suppose you are an extra in an upcoming movie. You will probably scrutinize that one scene where hundreds of people are milling around, just waiting for that two-fifths of a second when you can see the back of your head. Maybe your mom and your closest friend get excited about that two-fifths of a second with you ... *maybe*. But no one else will realize it is you. Even if you tell them, they won't care.

Let's take it a step further. What if you rent out the theater on opening night and invite all your friends and family to come see the new movie about you? People will say, "You're an idiot! How could you think this movie is about you?"

Many Christians are even more delusional than the person I've been describing. So many of us think and live like the movie of life is all about us.

Now consider the movie of life....

God creates the world. (Were you alive then? Was *God* talking to you when He proclaimed "It is good" about all He had just made?)

Then people rebel against *God* (who, if you haven't realized it yet, is the main character in this movie), and *God* floods the earth to rid it of the mess people made of it.

Several generations later, *God* singles out a ninety-nine-year-old man called Abram and makes him the father of a nation (did you have anything to do with this?).

Later, along come Joseph and Moses and many other ordinary and inadequate people that the movie is also not about. *God* is the one who picks them and directs them and works miracles through them.

In the next scene, *God* sends judges and prophets to His nation because the people can't seem to give Him the one thing He asks of them (obedience).

And then, the climax: The Son of *God* is born among the people whom *God* still somehow loves. While in this world, the Son teaches His followers what true love looks like. Then the Son of *God* dies and is resurrected and goes back up to be with *God*.

And even though the movie isn't quite finished yet, we know what the last scene holds. It's the scene I already described in chapter 1: the throne room of *God*. Here every being worships *God* who sits on the throne, for He alone is worthy to be praised.

From start to finish, this movie is obviously about God. He is the main character. *How is it possible that we live as though it is about us?*

Our scenes in the movie, our brief lives, fall somewhere between the time Jesus ascends into heaven (Acts) and when we will all worship God on His throne in heaven (Revelation).

We have only our two-fifths-of-a-second-long scene to live. I don't know about you, but I want my two-fifths of a second to be about my making much of God. First Corinthians 10:31 says, "So whether you eat or drink or whatever you do, do it all for the glory of God." That is what each of our two-fifths of a second is about.

So what does that mean for you?

Frankly, you need to get over yourself. It might sound harsh, but that's seriously what it means.

Maybe life's pretty good for you right now. God has given you this good stuff so that you can show the world a person who enjoys blessings, but who is still totally obsessed with God.

Or maybe life is tough right now, and everything feels like a struggle. God has allowed hard things in your life so you can show the world that your God is great and that knowing Him brings peace and joy, even when life is hard. Like the psalmist who wrote, "I saw the prosperity of the wicked.... Surely in vain have I kept my heart pure.... When I tried to understand all this, it was oppressive to me *till I entered the sanctuary of God*" (Ps. 73:3, 13, 16–17). It is easy to become disillusioned with the circumstances of our lives compared to others'. But in the presence of God, He gives us a deeper peace and joy that transcends it all.

To be brutally honest, it doesn't really matter what place you find yourself in right now. Your part is to bring Him glory—whether eating a sandwich on a lunch break, drinking coffee at 12:04 a.m. so you can stay awake to study, or watching your four-month-old take a nap.

The point of your life is to point to Him. Whatever you are doing, God wants to be glorified, because this whole thing is His. It is His movie, His world, His gift.

Thank God We Are Weak

So even though *God* has given us this life—this brief scene in His movie—we still forget we're not in control.

I was reminded of life's fragility by the birth of my fourth child and only son. All of a sudden our little girls wanted to carry their new baby brother around. My wife and I constantly told them to be careful because he's fragile. It got me wondering when he would no longer be fragile. When he's two? Eight? In junior high? College? Married? Once he has kids?

Isn't life always fragile? It is never under control. Even as I sat holding my son, I realized that I couldn't control whether he would love God.

Ultimately, I have just as little control over my own life and what will happen to me. Isn't the easiest thing at this point to start living in a guarded, safe, controlled way? To stop taking risks and to be ruled by our fears of what could happen?

Turning inward is one way to respond; the other is to acknowledge our lack of control and reach out for God's help.

If life were stable, I'd never need God's help. Since it's not, I reach out for Him regularly. I am thankful for the unknowns and that I don't have control, because it makes me run to God.

Just to put into perspective the brevity of our lives:

Throughout time, somewhere between forty-five billion and one hundred twenty-five billion people have lived on this earth.[4] That's

125,000,000,000. In about fifty years (give or take a couple of decades), no one will remember you. Everyone you know will be dead. Certainly no one will care what job you had, what car you drove, what school you attended, or what clothes you wore. This can be terrifying or reassuring, or maybe a mix of both.

Are You Ready?

As a pastor, I'm often called upon when life "vanishes like a mist." One of the most powerful examples I've seen of this was Stan Gerlach, a successful businessman who was well known in the community. Stan was giving a eulogy at a memorial service when he decided to share the gospel. At the end of his message, Stan told the mourners, "You never know when God is going to take your life. At that moment, there's nothing you can do about it. Are you ready?" Then Stan sat down, fell over, and died. His wife and sons tried to resuscitate him, but there was nothing they could do—just as Stan had said a few minutes earlier.

I'll never forget receiving that phone call and heading over to the Gerlach house. Stan's wife, Suzy, was just arriving home. She hugged me and cried. One of her sons, John, stepped out of the car weeping. He asked me, "Did you hear the story? Did you hear? I'm so proud of him. My dad died doing what he loved doing most. He was telling people about Jesus."

I was asked to share a word with everyone gathered. There were children, grandchildren, neighbors, and friends. I opened my Bible to Matthew 10:32–33: "Whoever acknowledges me before men, I will also acknowledge him before my Father in heaven. But whoever disowns me before men, I will disown him before my Father in heaven."

I asked everyone to imagine what it must have felt like for Stan. One moment, he was at a memorial service saying to a crowd, "This is who Jesus is!" The next, he was before God hearing Jesus say, "This is who Stan Gerlach is!" One second he was confessing Jesus; a second later, Jesus was confessing him!

It happens that quickly. And it could happen to any of us. In the words of Stan Gerlach, "Are you ready?"

Brooke Bronkowski was a beautiful fourteen-year-old girl who was in love with Jesus. When she was in junior high, she started a Bible study on her campus. She spent her babysitting money on Bibles so she could give them out to her unsaved friends. Youth pastors who heard about this brought her boxes of Bibles to give away.

Brooke wrote the following essay when she was about twelve; it will give you an idea of the kind of girl she was.

"SINCE I HAVE MY LIFE BEFORE ME"

By Brooke Bronkowski

> *I'll live my life to the fullest. I'll be happy. I'll brighten up. I will be more joyful than I have ever been. I will be kind to others. I will loosen up. I will tell others about Christ. I will go on adventures and change the world. I will be bold and not change who I really am. I*

will have no troubles but instead help others with their troubles.

You see, I'll be one of those people who live to be history makers at a young age. Oh, I'll have moments, good and bad, but I will wipe away the bad and only remember the good. In fact that's all I remember, just good moments, nothing in between, just living my life to the fullest. I'll be one of those people who go somewhere with a mission, an awesome plan, a world-changing plan, and nothing will hold me back. I'll set an example for others, I will pray for direction.

I have my life before me. I will give others the joy I have and God will give me more joy. I will do everything God tells me to do. I will follow the footsteps of God. I will do my best!!!

During her freshman year in high school, Brooke was in a car accident while driving to the movies. Her life on earth ended when she was just fourteen, but her impact didn't. Nearly fifteen hundred people attended Brooke's memorial service. People from her public high school read poems she had written about her love for God. Everyone spoke of her example and her joy.

I shared the gospel and invited those who wanted to know Jesus to come up and give their lives to Him. There must have been at least two hundred students on their knees at the front of the church praying for salvation. Ushers gave a Bible to each of them. They were Bibles that Brooke had kept in her garage, hoping to give out to all of her unsaved friends. In one day, Brooke led more people to the Lord than most ever will.

In her brief fourteen years on earth, Brooke was faithful to Christ. Her short life was not wasted. The words from her essay seem prophetic: *"You see, I'll be one of those people who live to be history makers at a young age."*

We've all been shocked to hear about or watch someone we know pass on from this life. Even as you read this, faces and names are probably coming to mind. It's good to think about those people in your life, and also to think about death. As the author of Ecclesiastes wrote, "It is better to go to a house of mourning than to go to a house of feasting, for death is the destiny of every man; the living should take this to heart" (7:2). Stories of people who died after living godly lives are stories with happy endings.

Sadly, many people die while living selfishly. Their funerals are filled by individuals who stretch the truth in order to create a semblance of a meaningful life. Nobody would dare say an unkind word at the funeral; there is an unspoken obligation to come up with something nice to say about the person who died. But sometimes we secretly think the same thing: *He really wasn't that great of a person.*

The truth is, some people waste their lives. This isn't meant to bash those who are gone, but rather to warn those who are alive.

I can pretty much guarantee you that your funeral will be nice. They all are. The fact is, at that point, you won't care. A. W. Tozer once said, "A man by his sin may waste himself, which is to waste that which on earth is most like God. This is man's greatest tragedy and God's heaviest grief."

When we face the holy God, "nice" isn't what we will be concerned with, and it definitely isn't what He will be thinking about. Any compliments you received on earth will be gone; all that will be left for you is truth. The church in Sardis had a great reputation, but it didn't matter. Jesus said to them, "I know your deeds; you have a reputation of being alive, but you are dead" (Rev. 3:1). All that matters is the reality of who we are before God.

> His work will be shown for what it is, because the
> Day will bring it to light. It will be revealed with fire,
> and the fire will test the quality of each man's work. If
> what he has built survives, he will receive his reward.
> If it is burned up, he will suffer loss; he himself will
> be saved, but only as one escaping through the flames.
> —1 Corinthians 3:13–15

Perhaps that sounds harsh, but harsh words and the loving truth often go hand in hand.

I think it's easy to hear a story like Brooke's and just move on, without acknowledging that it could just as easily be you or me or my wife or your brother whose life ends suddenly. You could be the next person in your family to die. I could be the next person at my church to die.

We have to *realize* it. We have to believe it enough that it changes how we live.

A friend of mine has a particularly wise perspective on this subject. He was asked if he weren't spending too much of his time serving and giving too much away. His gentle but honest response was, "I wonder if you'll say that after we're dead."

Friends, we need to stop living selfish lives, forgetful of our God. Our lives here are short, often unexpectedly so, and we can all stand to be reminded of it from time to time. That's why I wrote this chapter, to help us remember that in the movie of life, nothing matters except our King and God.

Don't let yourself forget. Soak it in and keep remembering that it is true. He is everything.

↓↑ CHAPTER THREE

crazy love

I was taught the song "Jesus Loves Me" as a young child: "Jesus loves me, this I know ..." Even if you didn't grow up in a church, you probably know how it ends: "... for the Bible tells me so."

If you've spent any time in church, you've heard expressed, in some form or another, the idea that God loves us. I believed this for years because, as the song puts it, "the Bible tells me so." The only problem is that it was a concept I was taught, not something I implicitly knew to be true. For years I "got" God's love in my head, checked the right answer on the "what God is like" test, but didn't fully understand it with my heart.

I don't think I'm the only person who has misunderstood God's love. Most of us, to some degree, have a difficult time understanding, believing, or accepting God's absolute and unlimited love for us. The reasons we don't receive, trust, or see His love vary from one person to the next, but we all miss out because of it.

For me, it had much to do with my relationship with my own father.

dad and DAD

The concept of being wanted by a father was foreign to me. Growing up, I felt unwanted by my dad. My mother died giving birth to me, so maybe he saw me as the cause of her death; I'm not sure.

I never carried on a meaningful conversation with my dad. In fact, the only affection I remember came when I was nine years old: He put his arm around me for about thirty seconds while we were on our way to my stepmother's funeral. Besides that, the only other physical touch I experienced were the beatings I received when I disobeyed or bothered him.

My goal in our relationship was not to annoy my father. I would walk around the house trying not to upset him.

He died when I was twelve. I cried but also felt relief.

The impact of this relationship affected me for years, and I think a lot of those emotions transferred to my relationship with God. For example, I tried hard not to annoy God with my sin or upset Him with my little problems. I had no aspiration of being wanted by God; I was just happy not to be hated or hurt by Him.

Don't get me wrong. Not everything about my dad was bad. I really do thank God for him, because he taught me discipline, respect, fear, and obedience. I also think he loved me. But I can't sugarcoat how my relationship with him negatively affected my view of God for many years.

Thankfully, my relationship with God took a major turn when I became a father myself. After my oldest daughter was born, I began to see how wrong I was in my thinking about God. For the first time I got a taste of what I believe God feels toward us. I thought about my daughter often. I prayed for her while she slept at night. I showed her picture to anyone who would look. I wanted to give her the world.

Sometimes when I come home from work, my little girl greets me by running out to the driveway and jumping into my arms before I can even get out of the car. As you can imagine, arriving home has become one of my favorite moments of the day.

My own love and desire for my kids' love is so strong that it opened my eyes to how much God desires and loves us. My daughter's expression of love for me and her desire to be with me is the most amazing thing. Nothing compares to being truly, exuberantly wanted by your children.

Through this experience, I came to understand that my desire for my children is only a faint echo of God's great love for me and for every person He made. I am just an earthly, sinful father, and I love my kids so much it hurts. How could I not trust a heavenly, perfect Father who loves me infinitely more than I will ever love my kids?

> If you, then, though you are evil, know how to give
> good gifts to your children, how much more will your
> Father in heaven give good gifts to those who ask him!
> —Matthew 7:11

God is more worthy of trust than anyone else, yet for so long I questioned His love and doubted His care and provision for me.

In Love with the One I Fear

If I could pick one word to describe my feelings about God in those first years of being a Christian, it would be *fear*. Basically, any verses that describe His overwhelming greatness or His wrath were easy for me to relate to because I feared my own father. I totally connected with passages like this one:

> He sits enthroned above the circle of the earth, and its people are like grasshoppers. He stretches out the heavens like a canopy, and spreads them out like a tent to live in. He brings princes to naught and reduces the rulers of this world to nothing. No sooner are they planted, no sooner are they sown, no sooner do they take root in the ground, than he blows on them and they wither, and a whirlwind sweeps them away like chaff.
>
> —Isaiah 40:22–24

Most Christians have been taught in church or by their parents to set aside a daily time for prayer and Scripture reading. It's what we are supposed to do, and so for a long time it's what I valiantly attempted. When I didn't, I felt guilty.

Over time I realized that when we love God, we naturally run to Him—frequently and zealously. Jesus didn't command that we have a regular time with Him each day. Rather, He tells us to "love the Lord your God with all your heart and with all your soul and with all your mind." He called this the "first and greatest commandment" (Matt. 22:37–38). The results are intimate prayer and study of His Word. Our motivation changes from guilt to love.

This is how God longs for us to respond to His extravagant, unending love: not with a cursory "quiet time" plagued by guilt, but with true love expressed through our lives. Like my little girl running out to the driveway to hug me each night because she loves me.

Fear is no longer the word I use to describe how I feel about God. Now I use words like *reverent intimacy*. I still fear God, and I pray that I always will. The Bible emphasizes the importance of fearing God. As we talked about in chapter 1, our culture severely lacks the fear of God, and many of us are plagued with amnesia. But for a long time, I narrowly focused on His fearsomeness to the exclusion of His great and abounding love.

Wanted

Recently, out of a desire to grow in my love for God, I decided to spend a few days alone with Him in the woods.

Before I left, a friend prayed, "God, I know how You've wanted this time with Francis…." Though I didn't say anything at the time, I secretly thought it was a heretical way to pray and that he was wrong to phrase it that way. I was going to the woods because I wanted more of God. But He's *God*; He certainly wouldn't want more of me! It seemed demeaning to think that God could long for a human being.

The more I searched the Scriptures, however, the more I realized my friend's prayer was right on, and that my reaction to his prayer indicated how much I still doubted God's love. My belief in God's love was still theoretical, not a reality I lived out or experienced.

I ended up spending four days in the woods without speaking to another human being. I had no plan or agenda; I just opened my Bible.

I don't think it was coincidence that on the first day it fell open to Jeremiah 1.

After reading that passage, I meditated on it for the next four days. It spoke of God's intimate knowledge of me. I had always acknowledged His complete sovereignty over me, but verses 4 and 5 took it to another level: "The word of the Lord came to me, saying, 'Before I formed you in the womb I knew you, before you were born I set you apart; I appointed you as a prophet to the nations.'"

In other words, God knew me before He made me.

Please don't skim over this truth just because you've heard it before. Take some time to really think about it. I'll say it again: *God knew you and me before we existed.*

When I first digested this, all of my other relationships seemed trivial by comparison. God has been with me from the start—in fact, from well *before* the start.

My next thought, alone in the woods, was that He determined what Jeremiah would do before he was even born. I questioned whether that was also true of me. Maybe all of this pertained only to Jeremiah's life?

Then I remembered Ephesians 2:10, which tells us that we were created "to do good works, which God prepared in advance for us to do." That verse is meant for me and all others who have been "saved by grace through faith." My existence was not random, nor was it an accident. God knew who He was creating, and He designed me for a specific work.

God's next words to Jeremiah assured me that I need not fear failure:

> "Ah, Sovereign Lord," I said, "I do not know how to speak; I am only a child."

But the Lord said to me, "Do not say, 'I am only a child.' You must go to everyone I send you to and say whatever I command you. Do not be afraid of them, for I am with you and will rescue you," declares the Lord. Then the Lord reached out his hand and touched my mouth and said to me, "Now, I have put my words in your mouth. See, today I appoint you over nations and kingdoms to uproot and tear down, to destroy and overthrow, to build and to plant."

—Jeremiah 1:6–10

When Jeremiah voices his hesitation and fear, God—the God of the galaxies—reaches out and touches his mouth. It's a gentle and affectionate gesture, something a loving parent would do. Through this illustration I realized that I don't have to worry about not meeting His expectations. God will ensure my success in accordance with His plan, not mine.

This is the God we serve, the God who knew us before He made us. The God who promises to remain with us and rescue us. The God who loves us and longs for us to love Him back.

So *why*, when we constantly offend Him and are so unlovable and unloving, does God persist in loving us?

In my childhood, doing something offensive resulted in punishment, not love. Whether we admit it or not, every one of us has offended God at some point. Jesus affirmed this when He said, "No one is good—except God alone" (Luke 18:19).

So why does God still love us, despite us? I do not have an answer to this question. But I do know that if God's mercy didn't exist, there would be no hope. No matter how good we tried to be, we would be punished because of our sins.

Many people look at their lives and weigh their sins against their good deeds. But Isaiah 64:6 says, "All our righteous acts are like filthy rags." Our good deeds can never outweigh our sins.

The literal interpretation of "filthy rags" in this verse is "menstrual garments" (think used tampons ... and if you're disgusted by that idea, you get Isaiah's point). It's hard to imagine something more disgusting that we could brag about or put on display. But compared to God's perfect holiness, that's how our good deeds appear.

God's mercy is a *free*, yet costly, *gift*. It cannot be earned. Our righteous acts, just like menstrual garments, certainly don't help us deserve it. The wages of sin will always be death. But because of God's mercy, sin is paid for through the death of Jesus Christ, instead of the death of you and me.

A Strange Inheritance

The very fact that a holy, eternal, all-knowing, all-powerful, merciful, fair, and just God loves you and me is nothing short of astonishing.

The wildest part is that Jesus doesn't *have* to love us. His being is utterly complete and perfect, apart from humanity. He doesn't need me or you. Yet He wants us, chooses us, even considers us His inheritance (Eph. 1:18). The greatest knowledge we can ever have is knowing God treasures us.

That really is amazing beyond description. The holy Creator sees you as His "glorious inheritance."

The irony is that while God doesn't need us but still wants us, we desperately need God but don't really want Him most of the time. He treasures us and anticipates our departure from this earth to be with Him—and we wonder, indifferently, how much we have to do for Him to get by.

Do I Have a Choice?

While I was speaking to some college students recently, an interesting twist on the contrast between our unresponsiveness and God's great desire for us came up. One student asked, "Why would a loving God force me to love Him?"

It seemed like a weird question. When I asked the student to clarify what he meant, he responded that God "threatens me with hell and punishment if I don't begin a relationship with Him."

The easy retort to that statement is that God doesn't force us to love Him; it's our choice. But there was a deeper issue going on, and I wasn't sure how to answer it in the moment.

Now that I've had time to think about it, I would tell that student that if God is *truly* the greatest good on this earth, would He be loving us if He didn't draw us toward what is best for us (even if that happens to be Himself)? Doesn't His courting, luring, pushing, calling, and even "threatening" demonstrate His love? If He didn't do all of that, wouldn't we accuse Him of being unloving in the end, when all things are revealed?

If someone asked you what the greatest good on this earth is, what would you say? An epic surf session? Financial security? Health? Meaningful, trusting friendships? Intimacy with your spouse? Knowing that you belong?

The greatest good on this earth is God. Period. God's one goal for us is Himself.

The Good News—the best news in the world, in fact—is that you can have God Himself. Do you believe that God is the greatest thing you can experience in the whole world? Do you believe that the Good News is not merely the forgiveness of your sins, the guarantee that you won't go to hell, or the promise of life in heaven?

The best things in life are gifts from the One who steadfastly loves us. But an important question to ask ourselves is this: Are we in love with God or just His stuff?

Imagine how awful it would feel to have your child say to you, "I don't really love you or want your love, but I *would* like my allowance, please." Conversely, what a beautiful gift it is to have the one you love look you in the eye and say, "I love you. Not your beauty, your money, your family, or your car. Just *you.*"

Can you say that to God?

Our love for Him always comes out of His love for us. Do you love this God who is everything, or do you just love everything He gives you? Do you really know and believe that God loves you, individually and personally and intimately? Do you see and know Him as Abba, Father?

Watch the online videos again at www.crazylovebook.com. It will remind you who you are and of the crazy, totally undeserved love of God.

profile of the lukewarm

*It is not scientific doubt, not atheism, not pantheism, not agnosticism,
that in our day and in this land is likely to quench the light of the gospel.
It is a proud, sensuous, selfish, luxurious, church-going,
hollow-hearted prosperity.*[5]

So there is an incalculable, faultless, eternal God who loves the frail
beings He made with a crazy kind of love. Even though we could die
at any moment and generally think our puny lives are pretty sweet
compared to loving Him, He persists in loving us with unending, out-
rageous love.

The only way I know to respond is like the man in one of Christ's
parables:

> The kingdom of heaven is like treasure hidden in a
> field. When a man found it, he hid it again, and then in
> his joy went and sold all he had and bought that field.
> —Matthew 13:44

In this account, the man joyfully sold all that he had so that he could obtain the only thing that mattered. He knew that what he had stumbled upon—the kingdom of heaven—was more valuable than anything he had, so he went for it with everything in him.

This kind of enthusiastic response to God's love is entirely appropriate. Yet what a contrast to our typical response at discovering the same treasure!

In the United States, numbers impress us. We gauge the success of an event by how many people attend or come forward. We measure churches by how many members they boast. We are wowed by big crowds.

Jesus questioned the authenticity of this kind of record keeping. According to the account in Luke chapter 8, when a crowd started following Him, Jesus began speaking in parables—"*so that*" those who weren't genuinely listening wouldn't get it.

When crowds gather today, speakers are extraconscious of communicating in a way that is accessible to everyone. Speakers don't use Jesus's tactic to eliminate people who are not sincere seekers.

The fact is, He just wasn't interested in those who fake it.

In the parable of the sower, Jesus explained that the seed is the truth (the Word of God). When the seed is flung onto the path, it is heard but quickly stolen away. When the seed is tossed onto the rocks, no roots take hold; there is an appearance of depth and growth because of the good soil, but it is only surface level. When the seed is spread among the thorns, it is received but soon suffocated by life's worries, riches, and pleasures. But when the seed is sown in good soil, it grows, takes root, and produces fruit.

My caution to you is this: *Do not assume you are good soil.*

I think most American churchgoers are the soil that chokes the seed because of all the thorns. Thorns are anything that distracts us from God. When we want God and a bunch of other stuff, then that means we have thorns in our soil. A relationship with God simply cannot grow when money, sins, activities, favorite sports teams, addictions, or commitments are piled on top of it.

Most of us have too much in our lives. As David Goetz writes, "Too much of the good life ends up being toxic, deforming us spiritually."[6] A lot of things are good by themselves, but all of it together keeps us from living healthy, fruitful lives for God.

I will say it again: *Do not assume you are good soil.*

Has your relationship with God actually changed the way you live? Do you see evidence of God's kingdom in your life? Or are you choking it out slowly by spending too much time, energy, money, and thought on the things of this world?

Are you satisfied being "godly enough" to get yourself to heaven, or to look good in comparison to others? Or can you say with Paul that you "want to know Christ and the power of his resurrection and the fellowship of sharing in his sufferings, becoming like him in his death" (Phil. 3:10)?

For a long time this verse had just too much Jesus for me. In my opinion, the verse should have ended after the word *resurrection*, so I could have an appealing, popular Jesus who didn't suffer. The feedback

I received from other Christians reassured me that this was a fine perspective, and it gave me little reason to strive to know Christ more deeply. I was told I was good enough, "godly enough."

But this went against everything I was reading in the Bible, so I eventually rejected what the majority said and began to compare all aspects of my life to Scripture. I quickly found that the American church is a difficult place to fit in if you want to live out New Testament Christianity. The goals of American Christianity are often a nice marriage, children who don't swear, and good church attendance. Taking the words of Christ literally and seriously is rarely considered. That's for the "radicals" who are "unbalanced" and who go "overboard." Most of us want a balanced life that we can control, that is safe, and that does not involve suffering.

Would you describe yourself as totally in love with Jesus Christ? Or do the words *halfhearted, lukewarm,* and *partially committed* fit better?

The Bible says to test ourselves, so in the next few pages, I am going to offer you a description of what halfhearted, distracted, partially committed, lukewarm people can look like. As you read these examples, I encourage you to take a searching, honest look at your life. Not who you want to be one of these days, but who you are now and how you are living today.

LUKEWARM PEOPLE attend church fairly regularly. It is what is expected of them, what they believe "good Christians" do, so they go.

"The Lord says: 'These people come near to me with their mouth and honor me with their lips, but their hearts are far from me. Their worship of me is made up only of rules taught by men'" (Isa. 29:13).

LUKEWARM PEOPLE give money to charity and to the church … as long as it doesn't impinge on their standard of living. If they have a little extra and it is easy and safe to give, they do so. After all, God loves a cheerful giver, right?

"King David replied to Araunah, 'No, I insist on paying the full price. I will not take for the Lord what is yours, or sacrifice a burnt offering that costs me nothing'" (1 Chron. 21:24).

"As he looked up, Jesus saw the rich putting their gifts into the temple treasury. He also saw a poor widow put in two very small copper coins. 'I tell you the truth,' he said, 'this poor widow has put in more than all the others. All these people gave their gifts out of their wealth; but she out of her poverty put in all she had to live on'" (Luke 21:1–4).

LUKEWARM PEOPLE tend to choose what is popular over what is right when they are in conflict. They desire to fit in both at church and outside of church; they care more about what people think of their actions (like church attendance and giving) than what God thinks of their hearts and lives.

"Woe to you when all men speak well of you, for that is how their fathers treated the false prophets" (Luke 6:26).

"I know your deeds; you have a reputation of being alive, but you are dead" (Rev. 3:1).

"Everything they do is done for men to see: They make their phylacteries wide and the tassels on their garments long; they love the place of honor at banquets and the most important seats in the synagogues; they love to be greeted in the marketplaces and to have men call them 'Rabbi'" (Matt. 23:5–7).

LUKEWARM PEOPLE don't really want to be saved from their sin; they want only to be saved from the penalty of their sin. They don't genuinely hate sin and aren't truly sorry for it; they're merely sorry because God is going to punish them. Lukewarm people don't really believe that this new life Jesus offers is better than the old sinful one.

"I have come that they may have life, and have it to the full" (John 10:10).

"What shall we say, then? Shall we go on sinning so that grace may increase? By no means! We died to sin; how can we live in it any longer?" (Rom. 6:1–2).

LUKEWARM PEOPLE are moved by stories about people who do radical things for Christ, yet they do not act. They assume such action is for "extreme" Christians, not average ones. Lukewarm people call "radical" what Jesus expected of all His followers.

"Do not merely listen to the word, and so deceive yourselves. Do what it says" (James 1:22).

"Anyone, then, who knows the good he ought to do and doesn't do it, sins" (James 4:17).

"What do you think? There was a man who had two sons. He went to the first and said, 'Son, go and work today in the vineyard.' 'I will not,' he answered, but later he changed his mind and went. Then the father went to the other son and said the same thing. He answered, 'I will, sir,' but he did not go. Which of the two did what his father wanted? 'The first,' they answered" (Matt. 21:28–31).

LUKEWARM PEOPLE rarely share their faith with their neighbors, coworkers, or friends. They do not want to be rejected, nor do they want to make people uncomfortable by talking about private issues like religion.

"Whoever acknowledges me before men, I will also acknowledge him before my Father in heaven.

But whoever disowns me before men, I will disown him before my Father in heaven" (Matt. 10:32–33).

LUKEWARM PEOPLE gauge their morality or "goodness" by comparing themselves to the secular world. They feel satisfied that while they aren't as hard-core for Jesus as so-and-so, they are nowhere as horrible as the guy down the street.

"The Pharisee stood up and prayed about himself: 'God, I thank you that I am not like other men— robbers, evildoers, adulterers—or even like this tax collector. I fast twice a week and give a tenth of all I get'" (Luke 18:11–12).

LUKEWARM PEOPLE say they love Jesus, and He is, indeed, a part of their lives. But only a part. They give Him a section of their time, their money, and their thoughts, but He isn't allowed to control their lives.

"As they were walking along the road, a man said to him, 'I will follow you wherever you go.' Jesus replied, 'Foxes have holes and birds of the air have nests, but the Son of Man has no place to lay his head.' He said to another man, 'Follow me.' But the man replied, 'Lord, first let me go and bury my father.' Jesus said to him, 'Let the dead bury their own dead, but you go and proclaim the kingdom of God.' Still another said,

'I will follow you, Lord; but first let me go back and say good-by to my family.' Jesus replied, 'No one who puts his hand to the plow and looks back is fit for service in the kingdom of God'" (Luke 9:57–62).

LUKEWARM PEOPLE love God, but they do not love Him with all their heart, soul, and strength. They would be quick to assure you that they try to love God that much, but that sort of total devotion isn't really possible for the average person; it's only for pastors and missionaries and radicals.

"Jesus replied: 'Love the Lord your God with all your heart and with all your soul and with all your mind.' This is the first and greatest commandment" (Matt. 22:37–38).

LUKEWARM PEOPLE love others but do not seek to love others as much as they love themselves. Their love of others is typically focused on those who love them in return, like family, friends, and other people they know and connect with. There is little love left over for those who cannot love them back, much less for those who intentionally slight them, whose kids are better athletes than theirs, or with whom conversations are awkward or uncomfortable. Their love is highly conditional and very selective, and generally comes with strings attached.

"You have heard that it was said, 'Love your neighbor and hate your enemy.' But I tell you: Love your enemies and pray for those who persecute you, that you may be sons of your Father in heaven. He causes his sun to rise on the evil and the good, and sends rain on the righteous and the unrighteous. If you love those who love you, what reward will you get? Are not even the tax collectors doing that? And if you greet only your brothers, what are you doing more than others? Do not even pagans do that?" (Matt. 5:43–47).

"Then Jesus said to his host, 'When you give a luncheon or dinner, do not invite your friends, your brothers or relatives, or your rich neighbors; if you do, they may invite you back and so you will be repaid. But when you give a banquet, invite the poor, the crippled, the lame, the blind, and you will be blessed. Although they cannot repay you, you will be repaid at the resurrection of the righteous'" (Luke 14:12–14).

LUKEWARM PEOPLE will serve God and others, but there are limits to how far they will go or how much time, money, and energy they are willing to give.

"'All these [commandments] I have kept since I was a boy,' he said. When Jesus heard this, he said to him, 'You still lack one thing. Sell everything you have and give to the poor, and you will have treasure in heaven. Then come, follow me.' When he heard this, he became very sad, because he was a man of great wealth. Jesus looked at him and said, 'How hard it is for the rich to enter the kingdom of God! Indeed, it is easier for a camel to go through the eye of a needle than for a rich man to enter the kingdom of God'" (Luke 18:21–25).

LUKEWARM PEOPLE think about life on earth much more often than eternity in heaven. Daily life is mostly focused on today's to-do list, this week's schedule, and next month's vacation. Rarely, if ever, do they intently consider the life to come. Regarding this, C. S. Lewis writes, "If you read history you will find that the Christians who did most for the present world were precisely those who thought most of the next. It is since Christians have largely ceased to think of the other world that they have become so ineffective in this."

"For, as I have often told you before and now say again even with tears, many live as enemies of the cross of Christ. Their destiny is destruction, their god is their stomach, and their glory is in their shame. Their mind is on earthly things. But our citizenship is in heaven. And we eagerly await a Savior from there, the Lord Jesus Christ" (Phil. 3:18–20).

"Set your minds on things above, not on earthly things" (Col. 3:2).

LUKEWARM PEOPLE are thankful for their luxuries and comforts, and rarely consider trying to give as much as possible to the poor. They are quick to point out, "Jesus never said money is the root of all evil, only that the *love* of money is." Untold numbers of lukewarm people feel "called" to minister to the rich; very few feel "called" to minister to the poor.

"Come, you who are blessed by my Father; take your inheritance, the kingdom prepared for you since the creation of the world.... I tell you the truth, whatever you did for one of the least of these brothers of mine, you did for me" (Matt. 25:34, 40).

"Is not this the kind of fasting I have chosen: to loose the chains of injustice and untie the cords of the yoke, to set the oppressed free and break every yoke? Is it not to share your food with the hungry and to provide the poor wanderer with shelter—when you see the naked, to clothe him, and not to turn away from your own flesh and blood?" (Isa. 58:6–7).

LUKEWARM PEOPLE do whatever is necessary to keep themselves from feeling too guilty. They want to do the bare minimum, to be "good enough" without it requiring too much of them.

They ask, "How far can I go before it's considered a sin?" instead of "How can I keep myself pure as a temple of the Holy Spirit?"

They ask, "How much do I have to give?" instead of "How much can I give?"

They ask, "How much time should I spend praying and reading my Bible?" instead of "I wish I didn't have to go to work, so I could sit here and read longer!"

"But who am I, and who are my people, that we should be able to give as generously as this? Everything comes from you, and we have given you only what comes from your hand" (1 Chron. 29:14).

"The kingdom of heaven is like treasure hidden in a field. When a man found it, he hid it again, and then in his joy went and sold all he had and bought that field. Again, the kingdom of heaven is like a merchant looking for fine pearls. When he found one of great value, he went away and sold everything he had and bought it" (Matt. 13:44–46).

LUKEWARM PEOPLE are continually concerned with playing it safe; they are slaves to the god of control. This focus on safe living keeps them from sacrificing and risking for God.

"Command those who are rich in this present world not to be arrogant nor to put their hope in wealth, which is so uncertain, but to put their hope in God, who richly provides us with everything for our enjoyment. Command them to do good, to be rich in good deeds, and to be generous and willing to share" (1 Tim. 6:17–18).

"Do not be afraid of those who kill the body but cannot kill the soul. Rather, be afraid of the One who can destroy both soul and body in hell" (Matt. 10:28).

LUKEWARM PEOPLE feel secure because they attend church, made a profession of faith at age twelve, were baptized, come from a Christian family, vote Republican, or live in America. Just as the prophets in the Old Testament warned Israel that they were not safe just because they lived in the land of Israel, so we are not safe just because we wear the label *Christian* or because some people persist in calling us a "Christian nation."

"Not everyone who says to me, 'Lord, Lord,' will enter the kingdom of heaven, but only he who does the will of my Father who is in heaven" (Matt. 7:21).

"Woe to you who are complacent in Zion, and to you who feel secure on Mount Samaria, you notable men of the foremost nation" (Amos 6:1).

LUKEWARM PEOPLE do not live by faith; their lives are structured so they never have to. They don't have to trust God if something unexpected happens—they have their savings account. They don't need God to help them—they have their retirement plan in place. They don't genuinely seek out what life God would have them live—they have life figured and mapped out. They don't depend on God on a daily basis— their refrigerators are full and, for the most part, they are in good health. The truth is, their lives wouldn't look much different if they suddenly stopped believing in God.

"And he told them this parable: The ground of a certain rich man produced a good crop. He thought to himself, 'What shall I do? I have no place to store my crops.' Then he said, 'This is what I'll do. I will tear down my barns and build bigger ones, and there I will store all my grain and my goods. And I'll say to myself, 'You have plenty of good things laid up for many years. Take life easy; eat, drink and be merry.'

But God said to him, 'You fool! This very night your life will be demanded from you. Then who will get what you have prepared for yourself?' This is how it will be with anyone who stores up things for himself but is not rich toward God" (Luke 12:16–21; see also Hebrews 11).

LUKEWARM PEOPLE probably drink and swear less than average, but besides that, they really aren't very different from your typical unbeliever. They equate their partially sanitized lives with holiness, but they couldn't be more wrong.

"Woe to you, teachers of the law and Pharisees, you hypocrites! You clean the outside of the cup and dish, but inside they are full of greed and self-indulgence. Blind Pharisee! First clean the inside of the cup and dish, and then the outside also will be clean. Woe to you, teachers of the law and Pharisees, you hypocrites! You are like whitewashed tombs, which look beautiful on the outside but on the inside are full of dead men's bones and everything unclean. In the same way, on the outside you appear to people as righteous but on the inside you are full of hypocrisy and wickedness" (Matt. 23:25–28).

This profile of the lukewarm is not an all-inclusive definition of what it means to be a Christian, nor is it intended to be used as ammunition to judge your fellow believers' salvation. Instead, as 2 Corinthians 13:5 says, it is a call to "examine yourselves, to see whether you are in the faith; test yourselves."

We are *all* messed-up human beings, and no one is totally immune to the behaviors described in the previous examples. However, there is a difference between a life that is characterized by these sorts of mentalities and habits and a life that is in the process of being radically transformed. We'll get to the transformation later, but now is the time to take a serious self-inventory.

When I was in high school, I seriously considered joining the Marines; this was when they first came out with commercials for "the few, the proud, the Marines." What turned me off was that in those advertisements, everyone was always running. Always. And I *hate* running.

But you know what? I didn't bother to ask if they would modify the rules for me so I could run less, and maybe also do fewer push-ups. That would've been pointless and stupid, and I knew it. Everyone knows that if you sign up for the Marines, you have to do whatever they tell you. They own you.

Somehow this realization does not cross over to our thinking about the Christian life. Jesus didn't say that if you wanted to follow Him you could do it in a lukewarm manner. He said, "Take up your cross and follow Me." He also said,

> Suppose a king is about to go to war against another
> king. Will he not first sit down and consider whether
> he is able with ten thousand men to oppose the one

coming against him with twenty thousand? If he is
not able, he will send a delegation while the other
is still a long way off and will ask for terms of peace.
In the same way, any of you who does not give up
everything he has cannot be my disciple.

—Luke 14:31–33

Jesus asks for everything. But we try to give Him less. Jesus said,

Salt is good, but if it loses its saltiness, how can it be
made salty again? It is fit neither for the soil nor for
the manure pile; it is thrown out.

—Luke 14:34–35

Jesus isn't just making a cute little analogy here. He is addressing
those who aren't willing to give everything, who won't follow Him all
the way. He is saying that lukewarm, halfhearted following is useless,
that it sickens our souls. He is saying that this kind of salt is not even
fit "for the manure pile."

Wow. How would you like to hear the Son of God say, "You would
ruin manure"?

When salt is salty, it helps manure become good fertilizer … but
lukewarm and uncommitted faith is completely useless. It can't even
benefit manure.

serving leftovers to a holy God

Of all the chapters in this book, this one was the hardest for me to write. I do not wish for my words to come across as controversial or difficult to swallow. But I had to write this chapter, because I believe what I'm about to talk about is important. And true.

In the last chapter we discussed various inappropriate responses to God's love. Now we are going to look at scriptural examples of poor responses to God's gift of love. Before you discount or ignore what I am about to say, read these passages objectively, without preconceived opinions staunchly in place.

My examination of lukewarm Christians in chapter 4 was by no means exhaustive. However, it did serve as a call to examine your heart in light of the points I listed. As I see it, a lukewarm Christian is an oxymoron; there's no such thing. To put it plainly, churchgoers who are "lukewarm" are not Christians. We will not see them in heaven.

In Revelation 3:15–18, Jesus says,

> I know your deeds, that you are neither cold nor hot. I wish you were either one or the other! So, because you are lukewarm—neither hot nor cold—I am about to spit you out of my mouth. You say, "I am rich; I have acquired wealth and do not need a thing." But you do not realize that you are wretched, pitiful, poor, blind and naked. I counsel you to buy from me gold refined in the fire, so you can become rich; and white clothes to wear, so you can cover your shameful nakedness; and salve to put on your eyes, so you can see.

This passage is where our modern understanding of *lukewarm* comes from. Jesus is saying to the church that because they are luke-warm, He is going to spit them out of His mouth.

There is no gentle rendering of the word *spit* in Greek. This is the only time it is used in the New Testament, and it connotes gagging, hurling, retching. Many people read this passage and assume Jesus is speaking to saved people. Why?

When you read this passage, do you naturally conclude that to be "spit" out of Jesus's mouth means you're a part of His kingdom? When you read the words "wretched, pitiful, poor, blind, and naked," do you think that He's describing saints? When He counsels them to "buy white clothes to wear" in order to cover their "shameful nakedness," does it sound like advice for those already saved?

I thought people who were saved were already made white and clothed by Christ's blood.

In an earlier draft of this chapter, I quoted several commentators who agreed with my point of view. But we all know that you can find quotes to support any view you want to take. You can even tweak word studies to help you in your effort. I'm not against scholarship, but I do believe there are times when we come to more accurate conclusions through simple reading.

And so I've spent the past few days reading the Gospels. Rather than examining a verse and dissecting it, I chose to peruse one gospel in each sitting. Furthermore, I attempted to do so from the perspective of a twelve-year-old who knew nothing about Jesus. I wanted to rediscover what reasonable conclusions a person would come to while objectively reading the Gospels for the first time. In other words, I read the Bible as if I'd never read it before.

My conclusion? Jesus's call to commitment is clear: He wants all or nothing. The thought of a person calling himself a "Christian" without being a devoted follower of Christ is absurd.

But please don't take my word for it. Read it yourself.

For years I struggled with the parable of the soils. I wanted to know if the person representing the rocky soil is saved, even though he has no root. I then wondered about the thorny soil: Is this person saved since he does have root?

I doubt if people even considered these questions back in Jesus's day! Is this idea of the non-fruit-bearing Christian something that we have concocted in order to make Christianity "easier"? So we can follow our own course while still calling ourselves followers of Christ? So we can join the Marines, so to speak, without having to do all the work?

Jesus's intention in this parable was to compare the only good soil to the ones that were not legitimate alternatives. To Him, there was one option for a true believer.

Let's face it. We're willing to make changes in our lives only if we think it affects our salvation. This is why I have so many people ask me questions like, Can I divorce my wife and still go to heaven? Do I have to be baptized to be saved? Am I a Christian even though I'm having sex with my girlfriend? If I commit suicide, can I still go to heaven? If I'm ashamed to talk about Christ, is He really going to deny knowing me?

To me, these questions are tragic because they reveal much about the state of our hearts. They demonstrate that our concern is more about going to heaven than loving the King. Jesus said, "If you love me, you will obey what I command" (John 14:15). And our question quickly becomes even more unthinkable: *Can I go to heaven without truly and faithfully loving Jesus?*

I don't see anywhere in Scripture how the answer to that question could be yes.

James 2:19 says, "You believe there is one God. Good! Even the demons believe that—and shudder." God doesn't just want us to have good theology; He wants us to know and love Him. First John 2:3–4 tells us, "We know that we have come to know him if we obey his commands. The man who says, 'I know him,' but does not do what he commands is a liar, and the truth is not in him."

Call me crazy, but I think those verses mean that the person who claims to know God but doesn't obey His commands is a liar and that the truth really isn't in him.

In Matthew 16:24–25, Jesus says, "If anyone would come after me, he must deny himself and take up his cross and follow me. For whoever wants to save his life will lose it, but whoever loses his life for me will find it." And in Luke 14:33, He says, "Any of you who does not give up everything he has cannot be my disciple."

Some people claim that we can be Christians without necessarily becoming disciples. I wonder, then, why the last thing Jesus told us was to go into the world, making *disciples* of all nations, teaching them to *obey all* that He commanded? You'll notice that He *didn't* add, "But hey, if that's too much to ask, tell them to just become Christians—you know, the people who get to go to heaven without having to commit to anything."

Pray. Then read the Gospels for yourself. Put this book down and pick up your Bible. My prayer for you is that you'll understand the Scriptures not as I see them, but as God intends them.

I do not want true believers to doubt their salvation as they read this book. In the midst of our failed attempts at loving Jesus, His *grace* covers us.

Each of us has lukewarm elements and practices in our life; therein lies the senseless, extravagant grace of it all. The Scriptures demonstrate clearly that there is room for our failure and sin in our pursuit of God. His mercies *are* new every morning (Lamentations 3). His grace *is* sufficient (2 Corinthians 12:9). I'm *not* saying that when you mess up, it means you were never really a genuine Christian in the first place. If that were true, no one could follow Christ.

The distinction is perfection (which none will attain on this earth) and a posture of obedience and surrender, where a person perpetually moves toward Christ. To call someone a Christian simply because he does some Christian-y things is giving false comfort to the unsaved. But to declare anyone who sins "unsaved" is to deny the reality and truth of God's grace.

From other references in Scripture (Colossians 2:1; 4:13, 15–16), the church at Laodicea appears to have been a healthy and legitimate church. But something happened. By the time Revelation was written, about twenty-five years after the letter to the Colossians, the Laodiceans' hearts apparently didn't belong to God—despite the fact that they were still active as a church. Their church was prospering, and they didn't seem to be experiencing any persecution.

They were comfortable and proud. Sounds familiar, doesn't it?

Poor Rich People

Ronnie, a blind boy who lives in eastern Uganda, is unique not because of his circumstances or the fact that he is blind, but because of his love for Jesus. If you were to meet Ronnie, one of the first things you would hear him say is, "I love Jesus so much, and I sing praises to Him every day!"

One of Ronnie's closest friends is a girl who is deaf. What stands out about these two isn't that they are handicapped or very poor, but that they are totally content and obviously in love with Jesus. They possess very little of what "counts" in our society, yet they have what matters most. They came to God in their great need, and they have found true joy.

Because we don't usually have to depend on God for food, money to buy our next meal, or shelter, we don't feel needy. In fact, we generally think of ourselves as fairly independent and capable. Even if we aren't rich, we are "doing just fine."

If one hundred people represented the world's population, fifty-three of those would live on less than $2 a day. Do you realize that if you make $4,000 a month, you automatically make *one hundred times* more than the average person on this planet? Simply by purchasing this book, you spent what a majority of people in the world will make in a week's time.

Which is more messed up—that we have so much compared to everyone else, or that we don't think we're rich? That on any given day we might flippantly call ourselves "broke" or "poor"? We are neither of those things. We are rich. Filthy rich.

Robert Murray M'Cheyne was a Scottish pastor who died at the age of twenty-nine. Although he lived in the early part of the nineteenth century, his words are astoundingly appropriate for today:

> I am concerned for the poor but more for you. I know not what Christ will say to you in the great day.... I fear there are many hearing me who may know well that they are not Christians because they do not love to give. To give largely and liberally, not grudgingly at all, requires a new heart; an old heart would rather part with its life-blood than its money. Oh my friends! Enjoy your money; make the most of it; give none away; enjoy it quickly for I can tell you, you will be beggars throughout eternity.[7]

The reality is that, whether we acknowledge our wealth or not, being rich is a serious disadvantage spiritually. As William Wilberforce once said, "Prosperity hardens the heart."

When talking to a wealthy person who wanted to go to heaven (and doesn't that describe most of us?), Jesus said, "'Sell everything you have and give to the poor, and you will have treasure in heaven. Then come, follow me.' When he [the rich man] heard this, he became very sad, because he was a man of great wealth. Jesus looked at him and said, 'How *hard* it is for the rich to enter the kingdom of God!'" (Luke 18:22–24). He says it's as hard as a camel to go through the eye of a needle—in other words, impossible. *But then* Jesus offers hopeful words: "What is impossible with man is possible with God" (v. 27).

In the very next chapter, as Jesus enters Jericho, we see exactly how the impossible becomes possible with God. There, the wealthy tax collector Zacchaeus gives half of his money to the poor and pays everyone back four times what he has defrauded them. And Jesus declares, "Today salvation has come to this house" (Luke 19:9).

The impossible happened that day—a rich man received salvation!

Offering Leftovers

God wants our best, deserves our best, and demands our best. From the beginning of time, He has been clear that some offerings are acceptable to Him and others are not. Just ask Cain, upon whose offering God "did not look with favor" (Gen. 4:5).

For years I gave God leftovers and felt no shame. I simply took my eyes off Scripture and instead compared myself to others. The bones I threw at God had more meat on them than the bones others threw, so I figured I was doing fine.

It's easy to fill ourselves up with other things and then give God whatever is left. Hosea 13:6 says, "When I fed them, they were satisfied; when they were satisfied, they became proud; then they forgot me." God gets a scrap or two only because we feel guilty for giving Him nothing. A mumbled three-minute prayer at the end of the day, when we are already half asleep. Two crumpled-up dollar bills thrown as an afterthought into the church's fund for the poor. Fetch, God!

> "But when you present the blind for sacrifice, is it not evil? And when you present the lame and sick, is it not evil? Why not offer it to your governor? Would he be pleased with you? Or would he receive you kindly?" says the Lord.
>
> —Malachi 1:8 NASB

The priests of Malachi's day thought their sacrifices were sufficient. They had spotless animals but chose to keep those for themselves and give their less desirable animals to God. They assumed God was pleased because they had sacrificed *something*.

God described this practice as *evil*.

Leftovers are not merely inadequate; from God's point of view (and lest we forget, His is the only one who matters), they're *evil*. Let's stop calling it "a busy schedule" or "bills" or "forgetfulness." It's called *evil*.

God is holy. In heaven exists a Being who decides whether or not I take another breath. This holy God deserves excellence, the very best I have. "But something is better than nothing!" some protest. Really, is it? Does *anyone* enjoy token praise? I sure don't. I'd rather you not say anything than compliment me out of obligation or guilt. Why would we think God is any different?

Two verses further on in Malachi, God says, "Oh that there were one among you who would shut the gates, that you might not uselessly kindle fire on My altar! I am not pleased with you, ... nor will I accept an offering from you" (NASB). God wanted the temple gates shut. The weak sacrifices of the laid-back priests were an insult to Him. He was saying that no worship is better than apathetic worship. I wonder how many church doors God wants to shut today.

Jesus's instruction to the people of the church at Laodicea was to buy from Him the things that really matter, the things they didn't even realize they needed. They were wealthy, but Jesus asks them to exchange their wealth for His gold that is refined through fire; they had clothing, but Jesus counsels them to buy clothes that were truly white and would cover their nakedness; they did not desire anything, but Jesus says they needed salve for their eyes that would cure their blindness. He asks them to give up what they thought was so necessary and valuable, in exchange for what really matters.

Mark Buchanan writes, "Physical sickness we usually defy. Soul sickness we often resign ourselves to."[8] The people in Laodicea did not realize or acknowledge that their souls were sick, that they were desperately in need of what Christ offered. As Tim Kizziar said, "Our greatest fear as individuals and as a church should not be of failure but of succeeding at things in life that don't really matter."

Recently I saw a bag of potato chips with a bold declaration splashed across the front: "Zero grams of trans fat." I was glad to know that I wouldn't be consuming any trans fat, which research has shown is detrimental to my health. But then I flipped the bag over and read the ingredients list, which included things like "yellow #6" and other artificial colors, and partially hydrogenated oil (which is trans fat, just a small enough amount that they can legally call it "0 grams"). I thought it was incredibly ironic that these chips were being advertised in a way that makes me think they are not harmful yet were really full of empty calories, weird chemicals, and, ironically, trans fat.

It struck me that many Christians flash around their "no trans fat" label, trying to convince everyone they are healthy and good. Yet they have no substantive or healthful elements to their faith. It's like the Laodiceans, who thought they had everything until Christ told them they were poor and wretched. They were all about declaring, "Look, we have no trans fat. We are wealthy, or we have good families, or we go to church every week." Obviously, it's not what you advertise that counts; it's what you are really made of.

God's definition of what matters is pretty straightforward. He measures our lives by how we love. In our culture, even if a pastor doesn't actually love people, he can still be considered successful as long as he is a gifted speaker, makes his congregation laugh, or prays for "all those poor, suffering people in the world" every Sunday.

But Paul writes that even if "I have all faith, so as to remove mountains, but have not love, I am nothing. If I give away all I have, and if I deliver up my body to be burned, but have not love, I gain nothing" (1 Cor. 13:2–3 ESV). Wow. Those are strong and unmistakable words. According to God, we are here to love. Not much else really matters.

So God assesses our lives based on how we love. But the word *love* is so overused and worn out. What does God mean by love? He tells us,

> Love is patient and kind; love does not envy or boast;
> it is not arrogant or rude. It does not insist on its
> own way; it is not irritable or resentful; it does not
> rejoice at wrongdoing, but rejoices with the truth.
> Love bears all things, believes all things, hopes all
> things, endures all things. Love never ends.... faith,
> hope, and love abide, these three; but the greatest of
> these is love.
>
> —1 Corinthians 13:4–8, 13 ESV

But even those words have grown tired and overly familiar, haven't they?

I was challenged to do a little exercise with these verses, one that was profoundly convicting. Take the phrase *Love is patient* and substitute your name for the word *love*. (For me, "Francis is patient....") Do it for every phrase in the passage.

By the end, don't you feel like a liar? If I am meant to represent what love is, then I often fail to love people well.

Following Christ isn't something that can be done halfheartedly or on the side. It is not a label we can display when it is useful. It must be central to everything we do and are.

If life is a river, then pursuing Christ requires swimming upstream. When we stop swimming, or actively following Him, we automatically begin to be swept downstream.

Or, to use another metaphor more familiar to city people, we are on a never-ending downward escalator. In order to grow, we have to turn around and sprint up the escalator, putting up with perturbed looks from everyone else who is gradually moving downward.

I believe that much of the American churchgoing population, while not specifically swimming downstream, is slowly floating away from Christ. It isn't a conscious choice, but it is nonetheless happening because little in their lives propels them toward Christ.

Perhaps it sounds as though I believe you have to work your way to Jesus. I don't. I fully believe that we are saved by grace, through faith, by the gift of God, and that true faith manifests itself through our actions. As James writes, "Faith by itself, if it is not accompanied by action, is dead" (2:17). The lives of many people who call themselves "Christians" in America lack manifestations of a vital and active faith.

And this, to be perfectly honest, frightens me. It keeps me up at night. It causes me to pray desperately and fervently for my congregation, for the groups of people I speak to, and for the church as a whole.

Henri Nouwen writes about this in his book *With Open Hands*: "It is hard to bear with people who stand still along the way, lose heart, and seek their happiness in little pleasures which they cling to.... You feel sad about all that self-indulgence and self-satisfaction, for you know with an indestructible certainty that something greater is coming."[9] Or, as Luke 9:25 says, "What good is it for a man to gain the whole world, and yet lose or forfeit his very self?"

How many of us would really leave our families, our jobs, our education, our friends, our connections, our familiar surroundings, and our homes if Jesus asked us to? If He just showed up and said, "Follow Me"? No explanation. No directions.

You could follow Him straight up a hill to be crucified. Maybe He would lead you to another country, and you would never see your family again. Or perhaps you would stay put, but He would ask you to spend your time helping people who will never love you back and never show gratitude for what you gave up.

Consider this carefully—have you ever done so? Or was your decision to follow Christ flippant, based solely on feelings and emotion, made without counting the cost?

What scares me most are the people who are lukewarm and just don't care. I think that if I did a poll of the readers of this book, many of you would say, "Yeah, I am definitely lukewarm at times, but I'm not really at a place to give more to God." Many of us believe we have as much of God as we want right now, a reasonable portion of God among all the other things in our lives. Most of our thoughts are centered on the money we want to make, the school we want to attend, the body we aspire to have, the spouse we want to marry, the kind of person we want to become.... But the fact is that *nothing* should concern us more than our relationship with God; it's about eternity, and nothing compares with that. God is not someone who can be tacked on to our lives.

Remember the visions from John and Isaiah of the throne room of God? Remember the pictures of the galaxies and how tiny we are in comparison? Remember the diversity of God, seen in the thousands of species of trees in the rainforest? We say to the Creator of all this magnitude and majesty, "Well, I'm not sure You are worth it.... You see, I really like my car, or my little sin habit, or my money, and I'm really not sure I want to give them up, even if it means I get You."

When we put it plainly like this—as a direct choice between God and our stuff—most of us hope we would choose God. But we need to realize that how we spend our time, what our money goes toward, and where we will invest our energy is equivalent to choosing God or rejecting Him. How could we think for even a second that something on this puny little earth compares to the Creator and Sustainer and Savior of it all?

We disgust God when we weigh and compare Him against the things of this world. It makes Him sick when we actually decide those things are better for us than God Himself. We believe we don't need anything Jesus offers, but we fail to realize that slowly, almost imperceptibly, we are drifting downstream. And in the process we are becoming blind, being stripped naked, and turning into impoverished wretches.

No wonder Jesus says He will spit lukewarm people out of His mouth!

Hear me clearly in this, because it is vital—in fact, there is nothing more important or eternal: *Are you willing to say to God that He can have whatever He wants? Do you believe that wholehearted commitment to Him is more important than any other thing or person in your life? Do you know that nothing you do in this life will ever matter, unless it is about loving God and loving the people He has made?*

If the answer to those questions is yes, then let your bet match your talk. True faith means holding nothing back; it bets everything on the hope of eternity.

I know that this whole swimming-upstream, pursuing-Christ, taking-up-your-cross, counting-the-cost thing isn't easy. It's so hard, in fact, that Jesus said the road is narrow and few will actually find it … and fewer still among those who are rich. Like the parable of the sower, don't assume you are the good soil; don't assume you are one of the few on the narrow way.

when you're in love

O God, I have tasted Thy goodness, and it has both satisfied me and made me thirsty for more. I am painfully conscious of my need for further grace. I am ashamed of my lack of desire. O God, the Triune God, I want to want Thee; I long to be filled with longing; I thirst to be made more thirsty still. Show me Thy glory, I pray Thee, so that I may know Thee indeed. Begin in mercy a new work of love within me. Say to my soul, "Rise up my love, my fair one, and come away." Then give me grace to rise and follow Thee up from this misty lowland where I have wandered so long.[10]

Have you ever met someone who was utterly and desperately in love with Jesus? I have. My wife's grandma Clara.

I spoke recently at Grandma Clara's funeral, and I could honestly tell the mourners gathered that I had never known anyone more excited to see Jesus. Every morning Clara would kneel by her bed and spend precious hours with her Savior and Lover; later in the day, just the sight of that corner of her bed would bring joy-filled tears and a deep anticipation of the next morning spent kneeling in His presence.

Grandma Clara acted toward God the way we act toward people we're madly in love with.

When you are truly in love, you go to great lengths to be with the one you love. You'll drive for hours to be together, even if it's only for a short while. You don't mind staying up late to talk. Walking in the rain is romantic, not annoying. You'll willingly spend a small fortune on the one you're crazy about. When you are apart from each other, it's painful, even miserable. He or she is all you think about; you jump at any chance to be together.

In his book *God Is the Gospel*, John Piper essentially asks whether we are in love with God:

> The critical question for our generation—and for every generation—is this: If you could have heaven, with no sickness, and with all the friends you ever had on earth, and all the food you ever liked, and all the leisure activities you ever enjoyed, and all the natural beauties you ever saw, all the physical pleasures you ever tasted, and no human conflict or any natural disasters, could you be satisfied with heaven, if Christ was not there?[11]

How many of you will read those words and say, "You know, I just might be okay with that"? If you are as deeply in love with God as Grandma Clara was, you know you could never be satisfied in a heaven without Christ.

Don't Try So Hard

My fear in writing the previous chapter is that it only evokes in you fear and guilt. Personal experience has taught me that actions driven by fear and guilt are not an antidote to lukewarm, selfish, comfortable living. I hope you realize instead that the answer is *love*.

Grandma Clara used to say, "I love love." Don't we all? Don't we crave it? And isn't that what God wants of us—to crave this relationship with Him as we crave all genuine love relationships? Isn't that what brings Him glory—when believers *desire* Him and are not merely slaves who serve Him out of obligation?

> You, my brothers, were *called to be free*. But do not use your freedom to indulge the sinful nature; rather, serve one another in love. The entire law is summed up in a single command: "Love your neighbor as yourself."
>
> —Galatians 5:13–14

Do you understand what this passage is saying? When we love, we're free! We don't have to worry about a burdensome load of commands, because when we are loving, we can't sin. Do you feel free in your Christian life?

In the same chapter, Paul writes, "The only thing that counts is faith expressing itself through love" (v. 6). Is loving God—and, by extension, loving people—what you are about? Is it what being a Christian means to you? Do you live as though faith, demonstrated through love, really is the only thing that counts?

For a long time, I sure didn't. And most of the people I knew were the same way.

There is so often a great disparity between how we feel about faith and how we are meant to feel. Why do so few people genuinely find joy and pleasure in their relationship with God? Why do most people feel they have to either pay God back for all He's done (buy His love) or somehow keep making up for all their inadequacies and failures (prove their love)? Why are the words of Psalm 63:1–5 not an honest reflection of our lives on most days?

> O God, you are my God, earnestly I seek you; my soul thirsts for you, my body longs for you, in a dry and weary land where there is no water. I have seen you in the sanctuary and beheld your power and your glory. Because your love is better than life, my lips will glorify you. I will praise you as long as I live, and in your name I will lift up my hands. My soul will be satisfied as with the richest of foods; with singing lips my mouth will praise you.

Lukewarm living and claiming Christ's name simultaneously is utterly disgusting to God. And when we are honest, we have to admit that it isn't very fulfilling or joyful to us, either.

But the solution isn't to try harder, fail, and then make bigger promises, only to fail again. It does no good to muster up more love for God, to will yourself to love Him more. When loving Him becomes obligation, one of many things we have to do, we end up focusing even more on ourselves. No wonder so few people want to hear from us about what we ourselves feel is a boring, guilt-ridden chore!

As I wrote in the last chapter, we are called to surrender everything for Christ—a concept most churchgoers are not particularly thrilled by. So what is missing? What's wrong with this picture? Are we just fooling ourselves that we really can be in love with God and that it is more satisfying than anything else? I don't believe so.

Help! I Don't Love You

God wants to change us; He died so that we could change.

The answer lies in *letting* Him change you. Remember His counsel to the lukewarm church in Laodicea? "Here I am! I stand at the door and knock. If anyone hears my voice and opens the door, I will come in and eat with him, and he with me" (Rev. 3:20). His counsel wasn't to "try harder," but rather to let Him in. As James wrote, "Come near to God and he will come near to you" (4:8).

Jesus Christ didn't die only to save us from hell; He also died to save us from our bondage to sin. In John 10:10, Jesus says, "I have come that they may have life, and have it to the full." He wasn't talking about the future. He meant now, in this lifetime.

The fact is, I need God to help me love God. And if I need His help to love Him, a perfect being, I definitely need His help to love other, fault-filled humans. Something mysterious, even supernatural must happen in order for genuine love for God to grow in our hearts. The Holy Spirit has to move in our lives.

It is a remarkable cycle: Our prayers for more love result in love, which naturally causes us to pray more, which results in more love....

Imagine going for a run while eating a box of Twinkies. Besides being self-defeating and sideache-inducing, it would also be near impossible—you would have to stop running in order to eat the Twinkies.

In the same way, you have to stop loving and pursuing Christ in order to sin. When you are pursuing love, running toward Christ, you do not have opportunity to wonder, *Am I doing this right?* or *Did I serve enough this week?* When you are running toward Christ, you are freed up to serve, love, and give thanks without guilt, worry, or fear. As long as you are running, you are safe.

But running is exhausting—if, that is, we are running from sin or guilt, out of fear. (Or if we haven't run in a while.) However, if we train ourselves to run toward our Refuge, toward Love, we are free—just as we are called to be.

As we begin to focus more on Christ, loving Him and others becomes more natural. As long as we are pursuing Him, we are satisfied in Him. It is when we stop actively loving Him that we find ourselves restless and gravitating toward other means of fulfillment.

When I read the Psalms, I witness an extreme intimacy that at times seems unattainable. I have to remind myself constantly that the Psalms were written by people just like me. They enjoyed closeness with God that you and I can experience. We should be communicating these words to Him:

Like a weaned child with its mother, like a weaned child is my soul within me. (Ps. 131:2)

You have filled my heart with greater joy than when their grain and new wine abound. I will lie down and sleep in peace, for you alone, O LORD, make me dwell in safety. (Ps. 4:7–8)

You have made known to me the path of life; you will fill me with joy in your presence, with eternal pleasures at your right hand. (Ps. 16:11)

The LORD is my strength and my shield; my heart trusts in him, and I am helped. My heart leaps for joy and I will give thanks to him in song. (Ps. 28:7)

Satisfy us in the morning with your unfailing love, that we may sing for joy and be glad all our days. (Ps. 90:14)

Your statutes are my heritage forever; they are the joy of my heart. (Ps. 119:111)

I don't want to make it sound deceptively easy; the Psalms are also filled with cries of pain:

Hear my prayer, O LORD, listen to my cry for help; be not deaf to my weeping. (Ps. 39:12)

Out of the depths I cry to you, O LORD; O Lord, hear my voice. Let your ears be attentive to my cry for mercy. (Ps. 130:1–2)

Jesus said, "In this world *you will have trouble*. But take heart! I have overcome the world" (John 16:33). Life isn't perfect when you follow Christ wholeheartedly; you will have trouble, Jesus says—it is pretty much guaranteed.

But He has overcome the world. So take heart, keep on, fight the good fight, pray continuously, and do not grow weary. There is nothing better than giving up everything and stepping into a passionate love relationship with God, the God of the universe who made galaxies, leaves, laughter, and me and you.

So what if I do believe that He has overcome the world? Until His kingdom comes, what about the sin I can't seem to escape? What about my messed-up family? What about my past? What about my grandma's cancer? What about the car accident that killed my friend? What about the divorce?

We each have a list that goes on and on.

The promise that our troubles are "achieving for us an eternal glory" seems hard to believe in the midst of the mess. It sounds trite to say that our struggles on this earth are "light and momentary," as Paul wrote, doesn't it? Mine don't feel that way. At times they threaten to engulf the rest of my life.

Yet God tells us that we are getting the better end of the deal, that we really will be rewarded in a manner that far outweighs our current frustrations and hardships. And even that we are blessed "when men hate you, when they exclude you and insult you and reject your name as evil, because of the Son of Man. Rejoice in that day and leap for joy, because great is your reward in heaven" (Luke 6:22–23).

> They called the apostles in and had them flogged. Then they ordered them not to speak in the name of Jesus, and let them go. The apostles left the Sanhedrin, rejoicing because they had been counted worthy of suffering disgrace for the Name. Day after day, in the temple courts and from house to house, they never stopped teaching and proclaiming the good news that Jesus is the Christ.
>
> —Acts 5:40–42

Wow. I hope that if I'm ever in a similar situation, I'll rejoice like the apostles did. But I sometimes think I would more likely lament my situation and get upset at God.

When I look at my relationship with God as a chore, a sacrifice, then *I* am getting the glory—not God. I keep saying, "Look what I have sacrificed for God...." or "Listen to what I do for God. It's hard, exhausting really...."

Instead, when we sacrifice, give, and even suffer, we can rejoice because we know that God rewards us. We are always the recipients of

His great and manifold gifts. Not the givers. Never the givers. David Livingston, a missionary to Africa during the 1800s, once said during a speech to students at Cambridge University, "People talk of the sacrifice I have made in spending so much of my life in Africa.… I never made a sacrifice. We ought not to talk of 'sacrifice' when we remember the great sacrifice which He made who left His Father's throne on high to give Himself for us."[12]

> The God who made the world and everything in it is the Lord of heaven and earth and does not live in temples built by hands. And he is not served by human hands, as if he needed anything, because he himself gives all men life and breath and everything else.
>
> —Acts 17:24–25

The Bible says that when we obey God's commands, we benefit. I think we naturally assume that if we look out for our own interests and concerns, we will be happy. But people who sacrifice for others will tell you that seasons of giving are the most rewarding of their lives.

It turns out that the Bible is right—"It is better to give than to receive" (Acts 20:35). People generally do find greater joy in giving freely to others than they do in rampant self-indulgence. Regarding this, the playwright George Bernard Shaw writes, "This is true joy in life, the being used up for a purpose recognized by yourself as a mighty one; the being a force of nature instead of a feverish, selfish little clod of ailments and grievances complaining that the world will not devote itself to making you happy."

God is the only true Giver, and He needs nothing from us. But still He wants us. He gave us life so that we might seek and know Him.

Jesus: Servant, Not Beggar

In Malachi 1:11 (NASB), God says, "From the rising of the sun even to its setting, My name will be great among the nations, and in every place incense is going to be offered to My name, and a grain offering that is pure; for My name will be great among the nations."

God tells the priests that if they don't want to give Him excellence, others will. God says His name will be great among the nations. Right now a hundred million angels are praising God's name; He certainly doesn't need to beg or plead with us. We should be the ones begging to worship in His presence.

Later in Malachi, we get an incredible promise from God: "'Bring the whole tithe into the storehouse, so that there may be food in My house, and test Me now in this,' says the LORD of hosts, 'if I will not open for you the windows of heaven and pour out for you a blessing until it overflows'" (Mal. 3:10 NASB).

This is the only place in the Bible where God invites His people to test Him, to try to out-give Him. He knows it is impossible, that no one can out-give the One from whom all things come. God knows people will realize that "we have given you only what comes from your hand" (1 Chron. 29:14). Nothing has strengthened my faith more than seeing God bless what I give back to Him, what I surrender at His feet.

If you really want to experience God's supernatural provision, then do as He says. Test Him. Give more than you can manage, and see how He responds.

When we are focused on loving Christ, it doesn't mean we do less. I used to do many of the same things I do now, but I was motivated by guilt or fear of consequences. When we work for Christ out of obligation, it *feels* like work. But when we truly love Christ, our work is a manifestation of that love, and it feels like love.

In reality, not one of us will ever be worthy. It *is* useless to attempt earning it; you will never feel ready. It is unknown and uncomfortable. But there really is a God who forgives everything and loves endlessly.

SomeOne I Can Be Real With

If you merely pretend that you enjoy God or love Him, He knows. You can't fool Him; don't even try.

Instead, tell Him how you feel. Tell Him that He isn't the most important thing in this life to you, and that you're sorry for that. Tell Him that you've been lukewarm, that you've chosen _____ over Him time and again. Tell Him that you want Him to change you, that you long to genuinely enjoy Him. Tell Him how you want to experience true satisfaction and pleasure and joy in your relationship with Him. Tell Him you want to love Him more than anything on this earth. Tell Him you want to treasure the kingdom of heaven so much that you'd willingly sell everything in order to get it. Tell Him what you like about Him, what you appreciate, and what brings you joy.

Jesus, I need to give myself up. I am not strong enough to love You and walk with You on my own. I can't do it, and I need You. I need You deeply and desperately. I believe You are worth it, that You are better than anything else I could have in this life or the next. I want You. And when I don't, I want to want You. Be all in me. Take all of me. Have Your way with me.

your best life... later

By now you've probably realized that you have a distinct choice to make: Just let life happen, which is tantamount to serving God your leftovers, or actively run toward Christ.

Do you recognize the foolishness of seeking fulfillment outside of Him? Do you understand that it's impossible to please God in any way other than wholehearted surrender? Do you grasp the beauty and deep joy of walking in genuine intimacy with God, our holy Father and Friend? Do you want to see God more than you desire security?

Maybe you answered yes to these questions but still wonder what that equates to, what the alternatives are to floating downstream or riding down the escalator. What does running toward Christ and pursuing Love look like in daily life?

The best place I know to look is in Scripture; here we gather wisdom and study the examples of those who followed God whole-heartedly. The best passage is probably Hebrews 11, a chapter often called the "hall of faith." It is tempting to assume that the people listed there were superhuman, or supersaints, and that you and I could never do the kinds of things they did.

But did you know that Abraham was afraid for his safety, so he lied about his wife, Sarah, and said that she was his sister ... twice? Consider Jacob, who stole his brother Esau's birthright, tricked his father into blessing him, and then fled in fear from Esau.

Or did you know that Moses was a murderer and so scared of speaking up that God had to send his brother, Aaron, to be Moses' mouthpiece? Also in Hebrews 11 we see Rahab, who was a Gentile and a woman (in that time, a serious disadvantage), not to mention a prostitute! Then there's Samson, who had so many issues I don't even know where to begin. And of course, David, a "man after God's own heart" who was an adulterer and a murderer, whose children were evil and out of control.

These people were far from perfect, yet they had faith in a God who was able to come through in seemingly dire situations. For example, Noah, who "by faith ... when warned about things not yet seen, in holy fear built an ark to save his family. By his faith he condemned the world and became heir of the righteousness that comes by faith" (Heb. 11:7). Noah spent 120 years building an ark and warning others of the impending judgment. Suppose the flood had never come—Noah would have been the biggest laughingstock on earth. Having faith often means doing what others see as crazy. Something is wrong when our lives make sense to unbelievers.

And then there's Abraham. Hebrews 11:17–19 says,

> By faith Abraham, when God tested him, offered
> Isaac as a sacrifice. He who had received the prom-
> ises was about to sacrifice his one and only son,
> even though God had said to him, "It is through
> Isaac that your offspring will be reckoned."
> Abraham reasoned that God could raise the dead,
> and figuratively speaking, he did receive Isaac back
> from death.

Abraham's hope lay in God's ability to raise the dead. What if
God hadn't stopped Abraham? Imagine standing over your dead
son after killing him. What would run through your mind as you
buried your child? Could you go on living as everyone called you
an insane murderer? These would have been the consequences of
Abraham's actions if God did not come through. But He did.

Finally, think about the martyrs. Hebrews 11:35–38 says,

> [They] were tortured and refused to be released, so
> that they might gain a better resurrection. Some
> faced jeers and flogging, while still others were
> chained and put in prison. They were stoned; they
> were sawed in two; they were put to death by the
> sword. They went about in sheepskins and goatskins,
> destitute, persecuted and mistreated—the world was
> not worthy of them. They wandered in deserts and
> mountains, and in caves and holes in the ground.

If eternity doesn't come and God does not exist, then, as Paul says, "If only for this life we have hope in Christ, we are to be pitied more than all men" (1 Cor. 15:19). If there is no God, then Paul and all the martyrs throughout history lived short lives full of needless suffering (2 Cor. 6:4–10).

But since God *is* real, Paul and the martyrs should be envied more than all people; their suffering was worth it. If we allow ourselves to live recklessly for Him, then we, too, will see His glory. We will see Him do the impossible.

Christians today like to play it safe. We want to put ourselves in situations where we are safe "even if there is no God." But if we truly desire to please God, we cannot live that way. We have to do things that cost us during our life on earth but will be more than worth it in eternity.

As chronicled in Hebrews 11, the God that the people of faith served is the very One we serve. As James 5:17 says, "Elijah was a man just like us." When you pray, your prayers are heard by the same God who answered Moses' prayer for water in the desert, the God who gave Abraham and his barren wife a son, and the God who made the slave Joseph second in power only to Pharaoh.

The ultimate example of sacrifice and surrender is, of course, Jesus Christ. He had everything and still chose to surrender it out of love for His Father. Your attitude should be the same as His....

Who, being in very nature God, did not consider
equality with God something to be grasped, but made
himself nothing, taking the very nature of a servant,
being made in human likeness. And being found
in appearance as a man, he humbled himself and
became obedient to death—even death on a cross!
Therefore God exalted him to the highest place and
gave him the name that is above every name, that at
the name of Jesus every knee should bow, in heaven
and on earth and under the earth, and every tongue
confess that Jesus Christ is Lord, to the glory of God
the Father.

—Philippians 2:6–11

John clearly tells us that "whoever claims to live in him must walk
as Jesus did" (1 John 2:6). Are you ready and willing to make yourself
nothing? To take the very nature of a servant? To be obedient unto
death? If your honest answer to those questions is yes, how are those
intentions manifested in your life?

In Matthew 25 we get a frightening picture of the coming judgment. In this passage, Christ condemns people to eternal punishment
because they did not care for Him during their lives on earth. "I was
hungry and you gave me nothing to eat, I was thirsty and you gave
me nothing to drink, I was a stranger and you did not invite me in, I
needed clothes and you did not clothe me, I was sick and in prison and
you did not look after me" (vv. 42–43).

The condemned protest, saying they never saw Christ in any
of these positions of need, and Jesus responds, "I tell you the truth,

whatever you did not do for one of the least of these, you did not do for me" (v. 45).

Ouch. To me that is like a stinging, unexpected slap in the face. Like many of you, I've heard that passage taught on numerous occasions. I've left convicted, but haven't taken it literally. We see it as a fresh perspective on poverty rather than a literal picture of impending judgment.

How would my life change if I actually thought of each person I came into contact with as Christ—the person driving painfully slow in front of me, the checker at the grocery store who seems more interested in chatting than ringing up my items, the member of my own family with whom I can't seem to have a conversation and not get annoyed?

If we believe that, as Jesus said, the two greatest commands are to "love the Lord your God with all your heart, soul, and mind" and to "love your neighbor as yourself," then this passage has a lot to teach us. Basically, Christ is connecting the command to "love God" with the command to "love your neighbor." By loving "the least of these," we are loving God Himself.

In this same chapter of Matthew, Jesus blesses some people for what they have done. Confused, they ask, "Lord, when did we see you hungry and feed you, or thirsty and give you something to drink? When did we see you a stranger and invite you in, or needing clothes and clothe you? When did we see you sick or in prison and go to visit you?" (vv. 37–39).

His answer is staggering: "The King will reply, 'I tell you the truth, whatever you did for one of the least of these brothers of mine, you did for me'" (v. 40). Jesus is saying that we show tangible love for God in how we care for the poor and those who are suffering. He expects us to treat the poor and the desperate as if they were Christ Himself.

Ask yourself this: If you actually saw Jesus starving, what would you do for Him?

> This is how we know what love is: Jesus Christ laid down his life for us. And we ought to lay down our lives for our brothers. If anyone has material possessions and sees his brother in need but has no pity on him, how can the love of God be in him? Dear children, let us not love with words or tongue but with actions and in truth. This then is how we know that we belong to the truth, and how we set our hearts at rest in his presence whenever our hearts condemn us.
>
> —1 John 3:16–20

In this passage, we see that John questions whether it is possible to truly have God's love in you if you have no compassion for the poor. He uses as his example Christ's love manifesting itself through the sacrifice of His very life.

God didn't just give a little for us; He gave His best. He gave Himself. John is saying that it is no different for us: True love requires sacrifice. And our love is shown by how we live our lives: "Let us not love with words or tongue but with actions and in truth."

One of the clearest ways we love "with actions and in truth" is through giving to others. By giving, I don't mean just money, although that is certainly an element of it.

Another important element of giving is with our time. Most of us are so busy that the thought of adding one more thing to our weekly schedule is stressful. Instead of adding in another thing to our lives, perhaps God wants us to give Him all of our time and let Him direct it as He sees fit. One of the most memorized verses in the whole Bible says, "For God so loved the world that he gave" (John 3:16). Right there we see the connection between loving and giving evidently established.

Giving that is not motivated by love is worth nothing. Paul says from this kind of giving we "gain nothing"; however, when we give out of love, we gain much. Giving results not only in heavenly compensation, but also gives us great joy in our lives here and now. As we love more genuinely and deeply, giving becomes the obvious and natural response. Taking and keeping for ourselves becomes unattractive and imprudent.

Remember the story where Jesus fed thousands of people with one boy's small lunch? In that story, according to Matthew, Jesus gave the loaves to His disciples and then the disciples passed them out to the crowd. Imagine if the disciples had simply held onto the food Jesus gave them, continually thanking Him for providing lunch for them. That would've been stupid when there was enough food to feed the thousands who were gathered and hungry.

But that is exactly what we do when we fail to give freely and joyfully. We are loaded down with too many good things, more than we could ever need, while others are desperate for a small loaf. The good things we cling to are more than money; we hoard our resources, our gifts, our time, our families, our friends. As we begin to practice regular giving, we see how ludicrous it is to hold on to the abundance God has given us and merely repeat the words *thank you*.

The apostle Paul addresses this issue of giving in light of the inequalities among the early believers:

> Our desire is not that others might be relieved while
> you are hard pressed, but that there might be equality.
> At the present time your plenty will supply what they
> need, so that in turn their plenty will supply what
> you need. Then there will be equality, as it is written:
> "He who gathered much did not have too much,
> and he who gathered little did not have too little."
> —2 Corinthians 8:13–15

Paul was asking the Corinthian believers to give to the impoverished saints in Jerusalem, the goal being that no one would have too much or too little. This idea is pretty far-fetched in modern-day culture, where we are taught to look out for ourselves and are thus rewarded.

The gap is so extreme in our world that we have to take lightly passages such as Luke 12:33: "Sell your possessions and give to the poor." How else can I walk out of a mud shack and back into my two-thousand-square-foot house without doing anything? The concept of downsizing so that others might upgrade is biblical, beautiful ... and nearly unheard of. We either close the gap or don't take the words of the Bible literally.

Dare to imagine what it would mean for you to take the words of Jesus seriously. Dare to think about your own children living in poverty, without enough to eat. Dare to believe that those really are your brothers and sisters in need.

Jesus said, "Whoever does the will of my Father in heaven is my brother and sister and mother" (Matt. 12:50). Do you believe that? Do you live like you believe it?

After hearing this truth preached, a guy at my church donated his house to the church and moved in with his parents. He told me that he will have a better house in heaven, and that it doesn't really matter where he lives during this lifetime. He is living like he believes.

Dream a little about what that might look like for you. Perhaps you start a movement called Aspiring to the Median, where people commit to living at or below the median U.S. income ($46,000 in 2006) and giving the rest away. Is it intimidating to think about giving radically and liberally?

I want to share a story with you. Anyone who has ever taken God at His word when He says, "Test me in this … and see if I will not … pour out so much blessing that you will not have room enough for it" (Mal. 3:10) probably has a similar tale.

A friend was faithfully giving 20 percent of his income to God, and suddenly his income dropped drastically. He knew he had to decide whether he should continue to give in a way that proved he trusted God. It wouldn't have been wrong to lower his giving to 10 percent. But my friend chose *instead* to increase his giving to 30 percent, despite the income reduction.

You can probably guess how the story ends. God blessed his faith and gave him more than enough, more than he needed. My friend got to experience God's provision firsthand.

When it's hard and you are doubtful, give more. Or, as Deuteronomy says, "Give liberally and be ungrudging when you do so, for on this account the LORD your God will bless you in all your work and in all that you undertake" (15:10 NRSV).

Maybe you have already made sacrifices. If so, you have seen that in some ways it gets easier, doesn't it? You have witnessed the benefits of giving and are blessed because of it. But it gets harder, too. The temptation to level off increases with each passing year. Pride tells you that you've sacrificed more than others. Fear tells you it's time to worry about the future. Friends say you've given enough, that it's someone else's turn now.

But Jesus says to keep on and you will see more of God. Do we really believe that "it ought to be the business of every day to prepare for our final day"?[13]

When Jesus sent out His twelve disciples (Luke 9:3), He told them to "take nothing for the journey—no staff, no bag, no bread, no money, no extra tunic." Why do you suppose He said this? Why not let them run home and grab a few supplies? Why not allow them to bring some money along just in case?

Jesus was forcing His disciples to trust Him. God would have to come through for them because they had nothing else to fall back on.

This place of trust isn't a comfortable place to be; in fact, it flies in the face of everything we've been taught about proper planning. We like finding refuge in what we already have rather than in what we hope God will provide. But when Christ says to count the cost of following Him, it means we must surrender everything. It means being willing to go without an extra tunic or a place to sleep at night, and sometimes without knowing where we are going.

God wants us to trust Him with abandon. He wants to show us how He works and cares for us. He wants to be our refuge.

↓↑

Walking in genuine intimacy and full surrender to God requires great faith. Hebrews 11:6 says, "Without faith it is impossible to please God, because anyone who comes to him must believe that he exists and that he rewards those who earnestly seek him."

Back when I was in Bible college, a professor asked our class, "What are you doing right now that requires faith?" That question affected me deeply because at the time I could think of nothing in my life that required faith. I probably wouldn't be living very differently if I didn't believe in God; my life was neither ordered nor affected by my faith like I had assumed it was. Furthermore, when I looked around, I realized I was surrounded by people who lived the same way I did.

Life is comfortable when you separate yourself from people who are different from you. That epitomizes what my life was like: characterized by comfort.

But God doesn't call us to be comfortable. He calls us to trust Him so completely that we are unafraid to put ourselves in situations where we will be in trouble if He doesn't come through.

Even though chapter 58 of Isaiah was written thousands of years ago, it speaks powerfully to the present day. I know it's long, but it is well worth the read, I promise.

> "For day after day they seek me out; they seem eager to know my ways, as if they were a nation that does what is right and has not forsaken the commands of its God. They ask me for just decisions and seem eager for God to come near them. 'Why have we fasted,' they say, 'and you have not seen it? Why have we humbled ourselves, and you have not noticed?'

"Yet on the day of your fasting, you do as you please and exploit all your workers. Your fasting ends in quarreling and strife, and in striking each other with wicked fists. You cannot fast as you do today and expect your voice to be heard on high. Is this the kind of fast I have chosen, only a day for a man to humble himself? Is it only for bowing one's head like a reed and for lying on sackcloth and ashes? Is that what you call a fast, a day acceptable to the LORD?

"Is not this the kind of fasting I have chosen: to loose the chains of injustice and untie the cords of the yoke, to set the oppressed free and break every yoke? Is it not to share your food with the hungry and to provide the poor wanderer with shelter—when you see the naked, to clothe him, and not to turn away from your own flesh and blood? Then your light will break forth like the dawn, and your healing will quickly appear; then your righteousness will go before you, and the glory of the LORD will be your rear guard. Then you will call, and the LORD will answer; you will cry for help, and he will say: Here am I.

"If you do away with the yoke of oppression, with the pointing finger and malicious talk, and if you spend yourselves in behalf of the hungry and satisfy the needs of the oppressed, then your light will rise in the darkness, and your night will become like the noonday. The LORD will guide you always; he will satisfy your needs in a sun-scorched land and will strengthen your frame. You will be like a well-watered garden, like a spring whose waters never fail. Your people will rebuild the ancient ruins and will raise up the age-old foundations; you will be called Repairer of Broken Walls, Restorer of Streets with Dwellings.

"If you keep your feet from breaking the Sabbath and from doing as you please on my holy day, if you call the Sabbath a delight and the LORD's holy day honorable, and if you honor it by not going your own way and not doing as you please or speaking idle words, then you will find your joy in the LORD, and I will cause you to ride on the heights of the land and to feast on the inheritance of your father Jacob." The mouth of the LORD has spoken.

—Isaiah 58:2–14

In verse 10, the phrase "if you spend yourselves" stands out to me even more than the amazing promises that follow. It reminds me of the parable of the talents in Matthew 25, wherein the servants are rewarded according to what they did with what they were given. It didn't seem to matter that one was given five talents and the other two. Both servants were faithful with what their master entrusted to them, and as a result both were rewarded liberally.

Similarly, we are each given different gifts and talents by our Master. The thing that matters most is how we use what we have been given, not how much we make or do compared to someone else. What matters is that we spend ourselves.

> And now, little children, abide in him, so that when he appears we may have confidence and not shrink from him in shame at his coming.
>
> —1 John 2:28 RSV

profile of the obsessed

Obsessed: *To have the mind excessively preoccupied with a single emotion or topic.*[14]

The idea of holding back certainly didn't come from Scripture. The Bible teaches us to be consumed with Christ and to faithfully live out His words. The Holy Spirit stirs in us a joy and peace when we are fixated on Jesus, living by faith, and focused on the life to come.

Lovers

I think sometimes we assume that if we are nice, people will know that we are Christians and want to know more about Jesus. But it really doesn't work that way. I know a lot of people who don't know Christ and are really nice people—nicer and more fun to be with, in fact, than a lot of Christians I know.

There has to be more to our faith than friendliness, politeness, and even kindness. Jesus teaches in Luke's gospel:

> If you love those who love you, what credit is that to you? Even "sinners" love those who love them. And if you do good to those who are good to you, what credit is that to you? Even "sinners" do that. And if you lend to those from whom you expect repayment, what credit is that to you? Even "sinners" lend to "sinners," expecting to be repaid in full. But love your enemies, do good to them, and lend to them without expecting to get anything back. Then your reward will be great, and you will be sons of the Most High, because he is kind to the ungrateful and wicked. Be merciful, just as your Father is merciful.
>
> —Luke 6:32–36

True faith is loving a person after he has hurt you. True love makes you stand out.

In October 2006, near Lancaster, Pennsylvania, a man stormed an Amish school and killed several girls. The day after the shootings, many Amish people visited the shooter's family to say they had forgiven him. That sort of forgiveness is incomprehensible to the world; because of it, people have even accused the families of being bad parents, of not dealing properly with their anger, of living in denial.

It is just this sort of love that is crazy to the world: true love, a kind found nowhere but through Christ.

We are commanded to love our enemies and do good to them. Who are your enemies? Or, in terms we connect with better, who are the people you avoid or who avoid you? Who are the people who have hurt you or hurt your friends or hurt your kids? Are you willing to do good to those people? To reach out to them?

Oftentimes, my first response when someone does something to me—or worse, to my wife or to one of my kids—is retaliation. I don't *want* to bless those who hurt me or people I love dearly. I wouldn't *want* to forgive someone who walked into my daughter's school and shot her and her friends.

But that is exactly what Christ asks us to do. He commands that we give without expecting anything in return.

Later in Luke, Jesus says,

> When you give a luncheon or dinner, do not invite your friends, your brothers or relatives, or your rich neighbors; if you do, they may invite you back and so you will be repaid. But when you give a banquet, invite the poor, the crippled, the lame, the blind, and you will be blessed. Although they cannot repay you, you will be repaid at the resurrection of the righteous.
>
> —Luke 14:12–14

Have you ever actually done anything like that? Do you give to those who cannot repay you? To those who would do you harm, if they could? To those who have already done you harm? This is Christ's love.

He gave us something for which we can *never* repay Him, and then He asks us to keep giving like He gives.

Frederick Buechner writes in *The Magnificent Defeat,*

> The love for equals is a human thing—of friend for friend, brother for brother. It is to love what is loving and lovely. The world smiles. The love for the less fortunate is a beautiful thing—the love for those who suffer, for those who are poor, the sick, the failures, the unlovely. This is compassion, and it touches the heart of the world. The love for the more fortunate is a rare thing—to love those who succeed where we fail, to rejoice without envy with those who rejoice, the love of the poor for the rich, of the black man for the white man. The world is always bewildered by its saints. And then there is the love for the enemy—love for the one who does not love you but mocks, threatens, and inflicts pain. The tortured's love for the torturer. This is God's love. It conquers the world.

People who are **obsessed** with Jesus give freely and openly, without censure. Obsessed people love those who hate them and who can never love them back.

Risk Takers

Haven't we all prayed the following prayer? *Lord, we pray for safety as we travel. We ask that no one gets hurt on this trip. Please keep everyone safe until we return, and bring us back safely. In Jesus's name we pray, amen.* The exact wording may vary a bit, but that is the standard prayer we recite before leaving on mission trips, retreats, vacations, and business trips.

We are consumed by safety. Obsessed with it, actually. Now, I'm not saying it is wrong to pray for God's protection, but I am questioning how we've made safety our highest priority. We've elevated safety to the neglect of whatever God's best is, whatever would bring God the most glory, or whatever would accomplish His purposes in our lives and in the world.

Would you be willing to pray this prayer? *God, bring me closer to You during this trip, whatever it takes....*

> People who are **obsessed** with Jesus aren't consumed with their personal safety and comfort above all else. Obsessed people care more about God's kingdom coming to this earth than their own lives being shielded from pain or distress.

Friends of All

Awhile back I had a free evening, so I decided to go to the store and buy some items to give away to those who needed them more than I do. It was a good idea, something I want my life to be characterized by more and more.

But it was embarrassing.

I realized that everyone I knew had enough, that I didn't know many people who were truly in need, and that I needed to change that. I needed to go and intentionally meet people who don't live like I do or think like I do, people who could never repay me. For their sake, but for my own as well.

First Timothy reaffirms that we are not to be controlled by money or to pursue it:

> Godliness with contentment is great gain. For we brought nothing into the world, and we can take nothing out of it. But if we have food and clothing, we will be content with that. People who want to get rich fall into temptation and a trap and into many foolish and harmful desires that plunge men into ruin and destruction. For the love of money is a root of all kinds of evil. Some people, eager for money, have wandered from the faith and pierced themselves with many griefs. But you, man of God, flee from all this, and pursue righteousness, godliness, faith, love, endurance and gentleness. Fight the good fight of the faith. Take hold of the eternal life to which you were called when you made your good confession in the presence of many witnesses.
>
> —1 Timothy 6:6–13

People who are **obsessed** with Jesus live lives
that connect them with the poor in some way
or another. Obsessed people believe that Jesus
talked about money and the poor so often
because it was really important to Him (1 John
2:4–6; Matt. 16:24–26).

Crazy Ones

Sometimes I feel like when I make decisions that are remotely biblical,
people who call themselves Christians are the first to criticize and say
I'm crazy, that I'm taking the Bible too literally, or that I'm not thinking about my family's well-being.

For example, when I returned from my first trip to Africa, I felt
very strongly that we were to sell our house and move into something
smaller, in order to give more away. The feedback I got was along the
lines of "It's not fair to your kids," "It's not a prudent financial choice,"
and "You are doing it just for show." I do not remember a single person
who encouraged me to explore it or supported the decision at the time.

We ended up moving into a house half the size of our previous
home, and we haven't regretted it. My response to the cynics, in the
context of eternity, was, am I the crazy one for selling my house? Or are
you for not giving more, serving more, being with your Creator more?

If one person "wastes" away his day by spending hours connecting
with God, and the other person believes he is too busy or has better
things to do than worship the Creator and Sustainer, who is the crazy
one? If one person invests her or his resources in the poor—which,

according to Matthew 25, is giving to Jesus Himself—and the other extravagantly remodels a temporary dwelling that will not last beyond his few years left on this earth, who is the crazy one?

When people gladly sacrifice their time or comfort or home, it is obvious that they trust in the promises of God. Why is it that the story of someone who has actually done what Jesus commands resonates deeply with us, but we then assume we could never do anything so radical or intense? Or why do we call it radical when, to Jesus, it is simply the way it is? The way it should be?

> **Obsessed** people are more concerned with obeying God than doing what is expected or fulfilling the status quo. A person who is obsessed with Jesus will do things that don't always make sense in terms of success or wealth on this earth. As Martin Luther put it, "There are two days on my calendar: this day and that day" (Luke 14:25–35; Matt. 7:13–23; 8:18–22; Rev. 3:1–6).

The Humble

The church in America loves to turn saints into celebrities, to make known the stories of humble people who have faithfully served Christ in some way. And there is much good that comes of that. In fact, in the next chapter we'll look closely at some examples.

But there can be a tragic consequence to it: Too many of these people fall for the praise and start to believe that they really are something special.

I spoke at a summer camp several years ago. Afterward, a number of students told me I was their "favorite speaker." It felt good to hear them talk about how funny and convicting my messages were. I loved it. I got back to my room and thanked God for helping me speak so well.

About three minutes into my prayer, I stopped. It hit me that the students were talking about *me*, not God. I was standing before a holy God and robbing Him of the glory that was rightfully His.

That's a terrifying position to find yourself in. God says, "I am the LORD; that is my name! I will not give my glory to another or my praise to idols" (Isa. 42:8). I realized immediately that any attention I received belonged to God.

It's pride, plain and simple, that keeps me from giving God all the glory and keeping some of it for myself. It is a battle we all fight, in some form or another, some of us daily or even hourly.

One of the ways I know to fight against pride is through focused prayer. What I mean is that before you say one word to God, take a minute and imagine what it would be like to stand before His throne as you pray. Remember the visions of John, in Revelation, and Isaiah; remember the many accounts of people coming into God's presence and how it always caused the people to fall on their faces in terror. And then start to pray.

A person who is **obsessed** with Jesus knows
that the sin of pride is always a battle.

> Obsessed people know that you can never be
> "humble enough," and so they seek to make
> themselves less known and Christ more known
> (Matt. 5:16).

Servers

As I shared in previous chapters, I used to be driven by my fear of God. I also used to work hard to prove that I was committed to God. Now I have tremendous fear and awe of God, but that doesn't motivate me. Now I work hard to serve God, but it isn't to prove my devotion.

Now I think I'm actually in love. Maybe that sounds corny to you, but I can't think of a more appropriate way to say it.

If a guy were dating my daughter but didn't want to spend the gas money to come pick her up or refused to buy her dinner because it cost too much, I would question whether he were really in love with her. In the same way, I question whether many American churchgoers are really in love with God because they are so hesitant to do anything for Him.

> People who are **obsessed** with Jesus do not
> consider service a burden. Obsessed people
> take joy in loving God by loving His people
> (Matt. 13:44; John 15:8).

Givers

Tears come to my eyes when I think about some of God's people I have had the privilege to meet in the past few years. These are people with families, with dreams, people who are made in God's image as much as you and I are. And these people are suffering.

Many of them are sick, some even dying, as they live out their lives in dwellings that we would not consider good enough for our household pets. I am not exaggerating. Much of their daily hardship and suffering could be relieved with access to food, clean water, clothing, adequate shelter, or basic medical attention.

I believe that God wants His people, His church, to meet these needs. The Scriptures are filled with commands and references about caring for the poor and for those who cannot help themselves. The crazy part about God's heart is that He doesn't *just* ask us to give; He desires that we love those in need *as much as we love ourselves*. That is the core of the second greatest command, to "love your neighbor as yourself" (Matt. 22:39).

He is asking you to love as you would want to be loved if it were your child who was blind from drinking contaminated water; to love the way you would want to be loved if you were the homeless woman sitting outside the café; to love as though it were your family living in the shack slapped together from cardboard and scrap metal.

Non-churchgoers tend to see Christians as takers rather than givers. When Christians sacrifice and give wildly to the poor, that is truly a light that glimmers. The Bible teaches that the church is to be that light, that sign of hope, in an increasingly dark and hopeless world. Matthew 5:16 says, "Let your light shine before men, that they may see your good deeds and praise your Father in heaven."

People who are **obsessed** with God are
known as givers, not takers. Obsessed people
genuinely think that others matter as much
as they do, and they are particularly aware of
those who are poor around the world (James
2:14–26).

Sojourners

Most Americans, and even more so those of us in Southern California,
think about life on earth way too much. Much of our time, energy,
and money are channeled toward that which is temporary. Paul writes,

> For, as I have often told you before and now say again
> even with tears, many live as enemies of the cross of
> Christ. Their destiny is destruction, their god is their
> stomach, and their glory is in their shame. Their mind
> is on earthly things. But our citizenship is in heaven.
> And we eagerly await a Savior from there, the Lord
> Jesus Christ, who, by the power that enables him to
> bring everything under his control, will transform our
> lowly bodies so that they will be like his glorious body.
> —Philippians 3:18–21

As I said before, my wife's grandma Clara offered a real-life
example of a person consumed with Jesus. I once attended a play
with my wife and some of her relatives, including Grandma Clara.

During intermission, I leaned over and asked what she thought of the play. She said, "Oh, honey, I really don't want to be here right now." When I asked why, she replied, "I just don't know if this is where I want to be when Christ returns. I'd rather be helping someone or on my knees praying. I don't want Him to return and find me sitting in a theater."

I was shocked by her answer. Yes, we are called to "keep watch" (Matt. 24:42), but it's strange to see someone who takes that command, and so many others, seriously. In fact, it's more than strange—it's convicting.

A person who is **obsessed** thinks about heaven frequently. Obsessed people orient their lives around eternity; they are not fixed only on what is here in front of them.

The Engrossed

Jesus didn't just pull the greatest command out of nowhere. He hearkened all the way back to the days of Moses, when God says to His people,

> Hear, O Israel: The LORD our God, the LORD is one. Love the LORD your God with all your heart and with all your soul and with all your strength. These commandments that I give you today are to be upon your

hearts. Impress them on your children. Talk about
them when you sit at home and when you walk along
the road, when you lie down and when you get up.
Tie them as symbols on your hands and bind them
on your foreheads. Write them on the doorframes of
your houses and on your gates.

—Deuteronomy 6:4–9

In Moses' time, the heart was understood to be the seat of a person's emotions, the very center of his being, the place where decisions
are made. The soul was considered the basis for a person's traits and
qualities, or his personality. Strength refers to physical, mental, *and*
spiritual strength.

So within this command to love God with "all your heart and with
all your soul and with all your strength," every fiber of humanity is
addressed. Our goal as people who follow Christ should be no less than
becoming people who are madly in love with God.

**A person who is obsessed is characterized by
committed, settled, passionate love for God,
above and before every other thing and every
other being.**

Unguarded Ones

Before my wife and I got married I knew that I had to tell her everything about me, all the ways I'd messed up, all the things I'd done. She

had to know what she was getting before she agreed to marry me. That conversation was not easy, but at the end of it, we still chose to be with each other, to commit our lives to one another.

I find myself acting differently with God. Often, when I pray, I will phrase my sentences in a way that makes me sound better. I will try to soften my sins, or touch up my true feelings before laying them before God. How foolish it is for me to be completely honest with my wife about my shortcomings, but try to fool God!

God wants us to be open with Him. He definitely doesn't want us to "season our wretchedness" as we would raw meat. He knows what we are, that we are disgusting, that all we are doing is trying to make ourselves feel better.

God desires true intimacy with each of us, and that comes only when we trust Him enough to be fully transparent and vulnerable.

> People who are **obsessed** are raw with God; they do not attempt to mask the ugliness of their sins or their failures. Obsessed people don't put it on for God; He is their safe place, where they can be at peace.

The Rooted

The average Christian in the United States spends ten minutes per day with God; meanwhile, the average American spends over four hours a day watching television.[15]

Perhaps TV is not your thing—maybe you don't even own one. But how about your time and your resources? How much of your money is spent on yourself, and how much is directed toward God's kingdom? How much of your time is dedicated to pursuing your life and your goals, and how much is focused on God's work and purposes?

God doesn't want religious duty. He doesn't want a distracted, halfhearted "Fine, I'll read a chapter ... now are You happy?" attitude. God wants His Word to be a delight to us, so much so that we meditate on it day and night.

In Psalm 1, He promises that those who do so are "like a tree planted by streams of water, which yields its fruit in season and whose leaf does not wither. Whatever he does prospers" (v. 3).

People who are obsessed with God have an intimate relationship with Him. They are nourished by God's Word throughout the day because they know that forty minutes on Sunday is not enough to sustain them for a whole week, especially when they will encounter so many distractions and alternative messages.

The Dedicated

Have you been in really good physical shape at some point in your life? If you aren't at that same level of fitness today, you probably know that it didn't "just happen"; you didn't lose your six-pack or your ability to run eight miles overnight. You stopped running regularly, or you quit lifting weights three times a week, or you started adding a couple of extra scoops of ice cream to your bowl. There are reasons that we are where we are and who we are, and they aren't random.

It is the same way with joy in our lives. We tend to think of joy as something that ebbs and flows depending on life's circumstances. But we don't just lose joy, as though one day we have it and the next it's gone, oh darn. Joy is something that we have to choose and then work for. Like the ability to run for an hour, it doesn't come automatically. It needs cultivation.

When life gets painful or doesn't go as we hoped, it's okay if a little of our joy seeps away. The Bible teaches that true joy is formed in the midst of the difficult seasons of life.

A person who is **obsessed** with Jesus is more concerned with his or her character than comfort. Obsessed people know that true joy doesn't depend on circumstances or environment; it is a gift that must be chosen and cultivated, a gift that ultimately comes from God (James 1:2–4).

Sacrificers

We cannot start believing that we are indispensable to God. According to the psalmist,

I have no need of a bull from your stall or of goats
from your pens, for every animal of the forest is mine,
and the cattle on a thousand hills. I know every bird
in the mountains, and the creatures of the field are
mine. If I were hungry I would not tell you, for the
world is mine, and all that is in it.... Sacrifice thank
offerings to God, fulfill your vows to the Most High.

—Psalm 50:9–12, 14

There is no way we can contribute or add to God. He has everything and is complete. When we are in God's presence, all we can do is
praise Him. Romans 11:35–36 says, "'Who has ever given to God, that
God should repay him?' For from him and through him and to him are
all things. To him be the glory forever! Amen."

A person who is **obsessed** with Jesus knows
that the best thing he can do is be faithful
to his Savior in every aspect of his life,
continually saying "Thank You!" to God. An
obsessed person knows there can never be
intimacy if he is always trying to pay God back
or work hard enough to be worthy. He revels in
his role as child and friend of God.

While these descriptions combined don't necessarily answer the question of what it looks like to be wholly surrendered to God, they represent important pieces of the puzzle. Hopefully you are beginning to imagine and pray about what this looks like in your own life.

who really lives that way?

Follow my example, as I follow the example of Christ.

—1 Corinthians 11:1

The stories that follow are true. They tell of people who sought to live their lives fully surrendered to God. Some are still alive; others have finished their race. Their examples differ vastly from one another, but each bears the mark of a person distinctly transformed by the beauty and reality of God's love and the guidance of the Holy Spirit.

In His letter to the church in Sardis, Jesus said, "You have a reputation of being alive, but you are dead. Wake up! Strengthen what remains and is about to die.... Yet you have a few people in Sardis who have not soiled their clothes. They will walk with me, dressed in white, for they are worthy" (Rev. 3:1–2, 4–5).

Jesus commended the few who were faithful. Likewise, there are a few in every generation who offer examples worth following.

Will your name be among the few that follow?

Nathan Barlow

A medical doctor who chose to utilize his skills in Ethiopia for more than sixty years, Nathan dedicated his life to helping people with mossy foot. Mossy foot is a debilitating condition primarily found in rural districts, on people who work in soil of volcanic origin. It causes swelling and ulcers in the feet and lower legs. The subsequent deformity, swelling, repeated ulcerations, and secondary infections make people with mossy foot social outcasts equivalent to lepers.[16]

I met Nathan shortly before he died. His daughter, Sharon Daly, attends my church and brought him to her home from Ethiopia when his health started to fail. After only a few weeks, he couldn't handle being in the States. The people he loved were still in Ethiopia, so his daughter flew him back home so he could spend his last days there.

Once, Nathan got a toothache, the pain of which was so intense that he had to fly away from the mission field to get medical attention. Nathan told the dentist that he didn't ever want to leave the mission field for the sake of his teeth again, so he had the dentist pull out *all* of his teeth and give him false ones so he wouldn't slow God's work in Ethiopia.

This amazing man was the first to help these outcasts, and he spent his life doing it. Yet he died quietly, without a lot of attention; no one really knew about him.

It surprised me that such a man of God would faithfully serve for so many years, despite minimal recognition. It is a beautiful thing to witness. The work Nathan started continues through his website, www. mossyfoot.com.

Simpson Rebbavarapu

Simpson was given his English name when he arrived at a missionary-run orphanage around the age of four. His parents had not yet named him, which happens often among the younger children of poverty-stricken, lower-caste families in India.

Simpson's mother was married as a child bride around the age of thirteen, a practice still common in Indian villages. Simpson was her sixth child, and the women in the village gave her herbs to end her pregnancy so that she wouldn't have to stop working *and* have another mouth to feed. But the herbs didn't work.

Other villagers suggested that she try the "English medicine." But when she went to the doctor to have him abort her baby, he did not come to work that day. So Simpson was born, and eventually his parents took him to the orphanage because they knew he would have a better life there, including an opportunity to be educated.

Simpson believes that God has always had His hand on his life, because if it had been up to his mother, he would never have been born. Currently, Simpson splits his time between an orphanage that he started and an evangelism ministry that brings God's Word to illiterate villagers through audio Bibles.

When asked how he lives and where he gets a salary, he answered in the most simple and humble manner, "I live by faith.… I don't have a family or a wife, so what do I need a salary for?" He would rather have that money go to supporting another program to help people or to expose more people to the Word of God.

Simpson says that by living this way, he has to trust that God has His hand on his life and will keep taking care of him. He also says his dependence keeps him in prayer and close to God. To learn more about what Simpson does, check out www.beumin.org.

Jamie Lang

When Jamie was twenty-three years old, she flew from the United States to Tanzania with $2,000 from her savings account. She planned to stay until she ran out of money, at which point she would come home.

Jamie was overwhelmed by all of the need that she encountered, so she started praying that God would allow her to make a radical difference in one person's life. After about six months, she met an eight-year-old girl at church who was carrying a baby on her back. Jamie learned that the baby's mother was dying from AIDS and that she was too weak to care for him. Jamie began to buy formula for the little boy, Junio, to provide him with the nutrition he desperately needed. At the time, he was half the size of a healthy baby.

Jamie fell in love with baby Junio. She wondered if she was being foolish—a barely twenty-four-year-old, single, white American enter-taining thoughts of adopting a baby. Besides, she didn't even know if Tanzania allowed international adoptions. Eventually, she discovered that the country *didn't* allow international adoptions; however, because she had lived there for over six months, she could establish residency.

Before Junio's mom died from AIDS, she came to Jamie and said, "I have heard how you are taking care of my son, and I have never known such a love. I want to be saved." Just before she died, she said, "I know that my son is taken care of, and I will see him in heaven someday."

Jamie spent six months going through the adoption process and then five more months working with the American embassy to get Junio a visa. When she finally came home, she had been gone for a year and a half.

Junio is now five years old, totally healthy, and HIV negative. When Junio's mom was pregnant with him, she took a "morning-after pill" late in her pregnancy in order to abort him. But instead it induced premature labor, and because Junio was so small, no bleeding occurred during his birth. Thus, he did not contract HIV from his mother. What was intended to end his life, God used to save it.

Since adopting Junio, Jamie has gotten married, had a little girl, and is moving back to Tanzania with her family to work with Wycliffe to translate the Bible for a group that has never heard it before.

Marva J. Dawn

Marva was born in Ohio in 1948. She is a lifelong scholar, having earned four masters degrees and a PhD. She is also a teaching fellow at Regent College in Vancouver, British Columbia, and is involved with the organization Christians Equipped for Ministry. Marva has written many books, is a gifted musician, and speaks to clergy and at conferences all over the world.

One of her books, *Unfettered Hope: A Call to Faithful Living in an Affluent Society*, specifically addresses what a faithful response looks like in our culture. Her life is a reflection of her belief that seemingly small acts of faithfulness can have a profound and significant impact on the world. All of the profits of her books go to support charities like Stand With Africa: A Campaign of Hope, which "supports African churches and communities as they withstand AIDS, banish hunger, and build peace."[17]

Marva and her husband live off his teacher's salary, which is not much. Despite Marva's many medical problems, she still refuses to take more money for herself. She cannot imagine spending to make her life more comfortable when so many people are desperate and dying throughout our world. She says that her 1980 Volkswagen Bug with its broken heater helps her focus more on prayer and to better identify with those in need.

Rich Mullins

Rich was born in 1955 in Richmond, Indiana, the third of six children. He began to study music at a young age and wrote his first song on the piano when he was just four years old.

Rich attended a Quaker church growing up, which later influenced his songwriting. He got his start writing songs for big-name recording artists, but in 1985 he recorded his debut album. For the next twelve years he made music, toured, and ministered to thousands of people through his simple yet weighty lyrics. His two most well-known songs are "Awesome God" and "Step by Step." His songs have been covered by artists and bands like John Tesh, Rebecca St. James, Michael W. Smith, Amy Grant, Third Day, Caedmon's Call, and Jars of Clay.

Despite his success in the music industry, Rich often ruffled the feathers of Christian music culture. He didn't consider music to be his primary purpose in life; to him, it simply enabled him to pursue the higher calling of loving people: children, his neighbors, enemies, and non-Christians. Sometimes he showed up to his concerts unshaven and barefoot. To keep others from putting him on a pedestal, he often confessed his sins and failures in public.

In 1995, Rich moved to a Navajo reservation in Arizona to teach music to the children who lived there. Rich never knew how successfully his albums sold because the profits from his concerts and albums went directly to his church. They paid him a small salary and gave the rest of the money away.

In September of 1997, Rich and a friend were driving to a benefit concert in Wichita, Kansas, when their Jeep flipped. Both men were thrown from the car; Rich was killed when a passing semi swerved to miss the Jeep and accidentally hit him. He was forty-one years old.

Rings

I don't know how old exactly Rings is, but he's definitely what you would call an old man. I also don't know where he was born or what his real name is; he simply goes by Rings. His home is the cab of his pickup, which he parks near downtown Ocean Beach, California. He is a chain smoker, an ex-convict, ex-addict, and ex-alcoholic.

Rings likes to say that if Jesus saved him, then Jesus is able to save anyone and everyone. So instead of using his monthly check to buy alcohol or a hotel room for himself, he spends all of it on food at the local supermarket. He transfers the food he buys to coolers in the back of his truck, then he drives to the beach and makes meals for his fellow homeless.

While preparing the food, Rings tells the gathering crowd about the freedom that Jesus brought into his life. He tells them that God is the One who told him to feed others with his money, and that it's because God loves each of them. This man gives everything he has to others—literally everything—because he knows he has nothing that wasn't given to him by God.

Rachel Saint

Rachel was born in 1914 in Pennsylvania, the only daughter among eight children. Her father was a stained-glass artist and their family often had very little food growing up.

When Rachel was eighteen, a kind, wealthy, elderly woman took Rachel on a trip to Europe and offered to make Rachel her heiress if she would be her companion for the rest of her life. While Rachel contemplated it, she knew she couldn't accept the offer of a comfortable life spent sipping tea and conversing.

After twelve years working at a halfway house for alcoholics, Rachel enrolled in linguistics school and became a missionary with Wycliffe Bible Translators in South America. She spent several years working with the Shapra Indians of Peru, but ultimately knew she was called to work with the Waorani Indians of Ecuador, who were notorious for spearing to death any outsiders immediately upon contact.

Eventually, Rachel was introduced to a Waorani woman, Dayuma, who agreed to teach Rachel the language of her people. For years Rachel studied the language and witnessed to Dayuma about Jesus Christ as she waited patiently for an opportunity to go to the Waorani without being killed. Rachel's own brother, Nate, a pilot for Mission Aviation Fellowship, had been killed by the Waorani people when they attacked him and four other missionaries. This only sharpened Rachel's desire to tell these people about the love of Christ.

After many years, Rachel finally went to meet and live with the Waorani people. She lived with them for twenty years. Over time, their culture of revenge and murder was transformed by hearing what they called "God's carvings" (the words of the Bible). The Waorani people became her family. They gave Rachel the Waorani name Nimu, which means "star."

Rachel eventually translated the New Testament into their language, and today she is buried with her people in Ecuador. At her funeral, a Waorani friend said, "She called us her brothers. She told us how to believe. Now she is in heaven…. God is building a house for all of us, and that's where we'll see Nimu again."

George Mueller

George was born in Prussia in 1805 and was attending the University of Halle when he became a Christian. Up until then he had been infamous for his gambling debts, drunken stories, and escapades. But his life was transformed when he came to know Christ.

He finished school and left for England to be a preacher. He and his British wife eventually settled in Bristol, England, where they saw many orphans roaming the streets—uncared for, unfed, often sick, and virtually guaranteed death at a young age. At this time, writers like Charles Dickens and William Blake had not yet brought attention to the plight of these children, and nothing was being done to help them.

George and his wife decided to start an orphanage that would be entirely free of charge, and for which they would never ask any money or support. When they had needs, they would go to God alone, trusting that He would give them everything they needed.

Many people were incredulous, and so the Muellers had two purposes in starting the orphanage: One was obviously to glorify God; the other was the spiritual welfare and temporal care of the fatherless and motherless children.

When the first orphan house opened, George and his wife, Mary, prayed for everything they needed. According to George's meticulous records, God provided all that they asked for. By the time George died, in 1898, over ten thousand orphans had been housed and cared for in the five orphan houses they built.

During his lifetime, a million and a half pounds went through George's hands in the form of donations. He directed every cent toward those in need. After his death, a British paper wrote of George that he "robbed the cruel streets of thousands of victims, the jails of thousands of felons, and the poorhouses of thousands of helpless waifs."[18] Another newspaper noted that it had all been accomplished by prayer alone.

Brother Yun

Yun was born in 1958 in the southern part of the Henan Province in China. When he was sixteen years old, with his father dying from stomach and lung cancer and his family nearly starving, Yun met Jesus Christ.

Over the years Yun grew and began to preach the gospel all over the country. The police were constantly tracking him and arrested him more than thirty times. Usually he was able to escape or elude long-term prison stays, but not always. Yun was imprisoned for three lengthy terms, including a four-year term during which he fasted from water and food for a period of seventy-four days. Although it is considered medically impossible for someone to survive that long without water, God sustained him. During those four years he underwent intense torture, including repeated beatings with a whip and multiple shocks from an electric baton.

Later on, Yun was held in a maximum-security prison in Zhengzhou. To ensure that he would never escape their prison, the guards beat Yun's legs until he was crippled. Despite this, Brother Yun walked out of the prison six weeks later. Gates and barriers that were always closed and barred were miraculously opened. No guard tried to stop him; it was as though he were invisible to them. It wasn't until he was outside and safe that Brother Yun realized he was walking on his "broken" legs!

Brother Yun and his family came to Germany in September 2001 after escaping China, where Yun is still wanted by the police. They now encourage believers around the world by sharing what God has done and is doing in China and many other places.

They are deeply involved with Back to Jerusalem, a movement aiming "to preach the gospel and establish fellowships of believers in all the countries, cities, towns, and ethnic groups between China and Jerusalem. This vision is no small task, for within those nations lay the three largest spiritual strongholds in the world today that have yet to be conquered by the gospel: the giants of Islam, Buddhism, and Hinduism."[19]

Shane Claiborne

Shane is in his late twenties and lives in The Simple Way community house in one of the worst neighborhoods in Philadelphia.

Shane and the other residents at The Simple Way work to expose structures that foster poverty and to imagine alternative ways to live. They take Christ's words in Matthew 25:40 literally when He said, "I tell you the truth, whatever you did for one of the least of these brothers of mine, you did for me." Their lives are about loving the very poor and broken in one of America's hardest cities. They do this in their own community as they feed hungry people, spend time with neighborhood children, run a community store, and reclaim decrepit blocks by planting community gardens.

Shane is a speaker at many conferences, churches, and events around the country. In keeping with the hospitality that characterized the early church, Shane stays with families when he agrees to speak. He doesn't ask for a specific honorarium, only that attendees give what they can to help support the ministries at The Simple Way.

When he travels, Shane asks those who hire him to lessen the ecological impact of his travel by biking to work, carpooling, or donating money to a worthy organization. All proceeds from Shane's book, *The Irresistible Revolution*, are given away.

In 2003, Shane went to Baghdad with the Iraq Peace Team (a project of Voices in the Wilderness and Christian Peacemaker Teams) for three weeks. Shane watched the U.S. invasion of Baghdad. While there, he visited the sites of the daily bombings, hospitals where the injured were taken, and families that had been devastated. He also attended worship services with Iraqi believers. To learn more about The Simple Way, visit www.thesimpleway.org.

The Robynson Family

This family of five, with three kids under the age of ten, chooses to celebrate the birth of Christ in a unique way. On Christmas mornings, instead of focusing on the presents under the tree, they make pancakes, brew an urn of coffee, and head downtown. Once there, they load the coffee and food into the back of a red wagon. Then, with the eager help of their three-year-old, they pull the wagon around the mostly empty streets in search of homeless folks to offer a warm and filling breakfast on Christmas morning.

All three of the Robynson kids look forward to this time of giving a little bit of tangible love to people who otherwise would have been cold and probably without breakfast. Can you think of a better way to start the holiday that celebrates the God who is Love?

Susan Diego

Now in her late forties, Susan grew up in a home where God was sought, and she has tried to obey Him her whole life. She has served Him in many ways, including working with high school students in her church youth group and at the public high school; teaching young mothers to be loving parents; raising four children of her own; starting a school; and opening her home as a place of rest for people of all ages and places in life.

When Susan was young, she told God that she would do anything He asked her to, but that she hated speaking in front of people and would prefer it not be that. However, recently Susan felt like God was moving her heart to speak and that she needed to say yes if an opportunity came up.

It did.

During spring break this year, Susan, her husband, and their two youngest children went to Uganda; there, Susan was in charge of leading a conference for the women. This meant speaking to hundreds of women at least ten different times, on numerous topics.

At first the thought of this terrified Susan. In fact, tears still come to her eyes when she talks about it. But she has submitted. She has said yes to God, to the one thing she hoped *never* to do.

Lucy

If you met Lucy at church, you would probably think she was somebody's innocent, dear grandmother. She is the kind of woman who will come and give you a huge hug and then introduce herself.

You would never guess that Lucy is an ex-prostitute. When she was in her teens and early twenties, drugs and prostitution dominated her life. Through an older Christian woman who reached out to the prostitutes, Lucy met Jesus and her life was completely transformed.

To this day, almost forty years later, Lucy lives near the same streets where she once worked as a prostitute and consistently opens her home to other young women who are caught in prostitution. It is common knowledge on the streets that if you need anything, you can come to Lucy's house. She doesn't have a lot, but her home is always open. Prostitutes, pimps, drug users, dealers, and anyone else who most people avoid—Lucy invites them in. This is her way of loving people who are in desperate need of the hope and love that Lucy found forty years ago.

Cornerstone Community Church

We started Cornerstone a little over thirteen years ago. The first few years, we gave about 4 percent of our budget away. As the years went by, we gave more and more money away.

This year we committed to giving away 50 percent of our budget. This is because we believe that when Jesus said to "love your neighbor as yourself," He wasn't kidding. If we really want to love our neighbors as ourselves, then it makes sense that we spend at least as much on them as we do on ourselves.

Another manifestation of our desire to love others is our new building plan. Initially, we had a beautiful plan for a new sanctuary that would have cost many millions of dollars. Now, however, we are in the process of getting permits to build an outdoor amphitheater that will seat plenty of people and save us about $20 million.

I'm sure there will be days when it's uncomfortable outside, but there will also be joy in knowing that we're sitting in the cold so that someone else can have a blanket.

Footnote about the Cornerstone Building Project

When I wrote the first edition of *Crazy Love*, the Cornerstone building project was moving forward. We were all inspired by the idea, and we had every intention of worshipping outdoors. But as it turns out, the project never came to fruition. This was largely due to opposition from city officials in the name of zoning laws.

But during the process, one of the elders asked me some questions that have stuck with me since: "Francis, would you really be content if we filled up the amphitheater a couple of times a weekend and had ten thousand people at the church? Would you be happy with that at the end of your life? Knowing you, I don't think you'd be content. Wouldn't it be better if you could help create a more reproducible model of church that wasn't so dependent on your speaking gift and limited to the size of a building?" It was very insightful, and it has caused us to head down this new path.

So we increased our focus on all of us living together as the church, rather than simply meeting together at the church. We wanted to take the focus off of a service and place it on church members meeting together throughout the week, meeting one another's needs, and serving and reaching their community. It wasn't easy, but the church became healthier through this process, and we decided that larger facilities weren't the pressing concern we thought they were.

I don't regret having gone through this process with Cornerstone—both the shift in philosophy and the struggle to make the new facilities happen were healthy for all of us—and the whole thing is a good reminder to hold our plans with an open hand. It's not about our strategies; it's about how the Spirit wants to lead and use us.

I hope these life stories have done more than encourage you; I hope they have eliminated every excuse for not living a radical, love-motivated life. I hope they have challenged the multitudes who "feel called to the rich" and ignore the poor. If biblical examples seem unattainable, hopefully these average, everyday people give you hope that you, too, can live a life worth writing about.

the crux of the matter

By now you're probably wondering, *What in the world does this mean for me?*

After the apostle Peter preached on the day of Pentecost, people "were cut to the heart and said ... 'Brothers, what shall we *do*?'" (Acts 2:37). The first church responded with immediate action: repentance, baptism, selling possessions, sharing the gospel.

We respond with words like *Amen, Convicting sermon, Great book* ... and then are paralyzed as we try to decipher what God wants of our lives. I concur with Annie Dillard, who once said, "How we live our days is ... how we live our lives." We each need to discover for ourselves how to live *this day* in faithful surrender to God as we "continue to work out [our] salvation with fear and trembling" (Phil. 2:12).

Should you put your house on the market today and downsize? Maybe. Should you quit your job? Maybe. Or perhaps God wants you to work harder at your job and be His witness there. Does He want you to move to another city or another country? Maybe. Perhaps He wants you to stay put and open your eyes to the needs of your neighbors. Honestly, it's hard enough for me to discern how to live my own life!

My suggestion as you think, make decisions, and discern how God would have you live is to ask yourself, "Is this the most loving way to do life? Am I loving my neighbor and my God by living where I live, by driving what I drive, by talking how I talk?" I urge you to consider and actually live as though each person you come into contact with is Christ.

Asking and reflecting on these sorts of questions points us in the right direction, but we have to get beyond asking the right questions. We often have "aha!" moments but don't act; in fact, we're famous for it in the church. Remember those retreat highs followed by the inevitable lull? Or the excitement you felt on your first mission trip but forgot shortly after returning home? Memories are wonderful, but do you live differently because of them?

The stories in chapter 9 are brief snapshots of how a few people have lived out true Christianity in America and around the world. Their lives are a challenge of the status quo and examples of a different way to live.

The point is that there *is* another path, an alternative to the individualism, selfishness, and materialism of the American Dream (even the so-called Christian version). I hope their stories reminded you that God works in a vast number of ways, that He has more in store for you than you can really imagine right now.

A Nike commercial ran years ago, featuring the first-draft pick into the NBA, Harold Miner. In the commercial, he said something like, "Some people ask if I'm going to be the next Magic Johnson, the next Larry Bird, or the next Michael Jordan. I tell them, I'm going to be the first Harold Miner." He ended up having a miserable career in the NBA, but it was still a cool commercial. And his point—to be yourself—was valid.

Oswald Chambers writes, "Never make a principle out of your experience; let God be as original with other people as He is with you."[20] To that I would add, "Be careful not to turn others' lives into the mold for your own." Allow God to be as creative with you as He is with each of us.

Have you ever said, "I was made for this moment"? Do you believe you were crafted for specific good works, things that God knew before you even existed? Or do you compare your life to others and lament what you have been given?

We have a God who is a Creator, not a duplicator. He's never made a Francis Chan before. Paul tells us,

> There are different kinds of gifts, but the same Spirit. There are different kinds of service, but the same Lord. There are different kinds of working, but the same God works all of them in all men. Now to each one the manifestation of the Spirit is given for the common good.
>
> —1 Corinthians 12:4–7

Imagine if you opened up a drawer in your kitchen and found twenty cheese graters but no other utensils. Not very helpful when you're looking for something to eat your soup with. Just as there are different utensils in the kitchen that serve diverse functions, God has created unique people to accomplish a variety of purposes throughout the world.

That is why I cannot say in this book, "Everyone is supposed to be a missionary" or "You need to sell your car and start taking public transportation." What I *can* say is that you must learn to listen to and obey God, especially in a society where it's easy and expected to do what is most comfortable.

I wrote this book because much of our talk doesn't match our lives. We say things like, "I can do all things through Christ who strengthens me," and "Trust in the Lord with all your heart." Then we live and plan like we don't believe God even exists. We try to set our lives up so everything will be fine even if God doesn't come through. But true faith means holding nothing back. It means putting every hope in God's fidelity to His promises.

A friend of mine once said that Christians are like manure: Spread them out and they help everything grow better, but keep them in one big pile and they stink horribly. Which are you? The kind that reeks, around which people walk a wide swath? Or the kind that trusts God enough to let Him spread you out—whether that means going outside your normal group of Christian friends, increasing your material giving, or using your time to serve others?

I was convicted by my lack of faith in college. I realized that my choices had situated me in a pile of stinking manure, and this motivated me to put myself in uncomfortable situations. I began going into downtown Los Angeles to share my faith. I didn't "hear God calling me" to drive downtown; I just chose to go. I obeyed.

Most of us use "I'm waiting for God to reveal His calling on my life" as a means of avoiding action. Did you hear God calling you to sit in front of the television yesterday? Or to go on your last vacation? Or exercise this morning? Probably not, but you still did it. The point isn't that vacations or exercise are wrong, but that we are quick to rationalize our entertainment and priorities yet are slow to commit to serving God.

A friend of mine was speaking recently. Afterward a guy came up and told him, "I would go serve God as a missionary overseas, but, honestly, if I went right now it would only be out of obedience." My friend's response was "Yes, and …?"

Jesus said, "If you love me, you will obey what I command" (John 14:15). Jesus did not say, "If you love me you will obey me when you feel called or good about doing so…." If we love, then we obey. Period. This sort of matter-of-fact obedience is part of what it means to live a life of faith.

The greatest blessing I received during those trips to the inner city was seeing God work in situations where He has to. As a result, I've made it a commitment to consistently put myself in situations that scare me and require God to come through. When I survey my life, I realize that *those* times have been the most meaningful and satisfying of my life. They were the times when I truly experienced life and God.

For so much of my life I didn't understand the desirability of God or trust in His love enough to submit my hopes and dreams. I lived in a constant state of trying to be "devoted enough" to Him, yet I never quite made it.

I knew God wanted all of me, yet I feared what complete surrender to Him would mean. Trying harder doesn't work for me. Slowly I've learned to pray for God's help, and He has become my greatest love and desire.

Despite this huge shift in focus and tone in my relationship with God, I still struggle to stay focused on Jesus every day. But a couple of things help me keep going.

First, I remember that if I stop pursuing Christ, I am letting our relationship deteriorate. We never grow closer to God when we just live life; it takes deliberate pursuit and attentiveness. When I pray, I sometimes ask God to make it the most intimate time of prayer I've *ever* had. Many times when I speak, whether at my church or another venue, I remind myself that I could die right after I finish, so what would I want my last words to be?

Second, I remember that we are not alone. Even now there are thousands of beings in heaven watching what is going on down here—a "great cloud of witnesses," the Scripture says. It reminds me that there is so much more to our existence than what we can see. What we do reverberates through the heavens and into eternity.

Try for a whole day to be conscious of heaven. Realize that so much is going on outside of this dimension and our existence. God and His angels are watching, even now.

What really keeps me going is the gift and power we have been given in the Holy Spirit. Before Christ left this earth, He told His disciples,

> I tell you the truth: It is for your good that I am going away. Unless I go away, the Counselor will not come to you; but if I go, I will send him to you. When he comes, he will convict the world of guilt in regard to sin and righteousness and judgment.... When he, the Spirit of truth, comes, he will guide you into all truth.
>
> —John 16:7–8, 13

The disciples must have been shocked by the idea that it was for their good that Jesus was leaving. What could possibly be better than having Jesus by your side? Wouldn't you rather have Jesus physically walking next to you all day than have the seemingly elusive Holy Spirit living in you?

Our view of the Holy Spirit is too small. The Holy Spirit is the One who changes the church, but we have to remember that the Holy Spirit lives in us. It is individual people living Spirit-filled lives that will change the church.

Ephesians 5:18 says, "Be filled with the Spirit." If you look at the Greek, it is written as both a present imperative (a continual command) and in the passive voice. The imperative part means that being filled with the Spirit isn't something we do once; rather, it is something we do always and repeatedly. And the passive element communicates God's necessary action in the process of filling.

I have never been more excited about the church. I think there is tremendous reason to expect good things. At the beginning of this chapter, I mentioned how Annie Dillard wrote that the way we live out our days is the way we will live our lives. It's similar with the body of Christ: How we believers live out our lives is a microcosm of the life of the church.

My hope and prayer is that you finish this book with hope, believing that part of your responsibility in the body of Christ is to help set the pace for the church by listening and obeying and *living* Christ. Knowing that God has called us each to live faithful and devoted lives before Him, by the power of His Spirit. You do not need to preach to your pastor or congregation; you simply need to live out in your daily life the love and obedience that God has asked of you.

I was recently told about a man who heard me preach on 1 Corinthians 15:19–20, where Paul writes, "If only for this life we have hope in Christ, we are to be pitied more than all men. But Christ has indeed been raised from the dead." This man was convicted that since Christ is indeed alive, he needed to live like it. So he quit his well-paying job and became a pastor—something he had felt called to do for a while.

When people make changes in their lives like this, it carries greater impact than when they merely make impassioned declarations. The world needs Christians who don't tolerate the complacency of their own lives.

Is This What I Want to Be Doing When Christ Comes Back?

And so we are at the end of this book. I don't think it's coincidence that God has encouraged my heart so much over this past week with the story of the three believers who were martyred in Turkey.

I'm writing this in April 2007, and the news about the three martyrs—Tilman, Necati, and Ugur—is still fresh. I can't get them out of my mind. They were tortured for three hours in ways that I didn't know were humanly possible. I'll spare you the details, but it was repulsive and horrific. I think of how they must have looked at each other while being tortured with stares that said, "Just hold on a little longer. Don't deny Him! It'll all be worth it."

It's been about a week and a half since their deaths. How thrilled they must be right now—I cannot imagine the joy they felt just five seconds after their deaths. I know that when I meet them, they'll say it was so worth it. A hundred or thousand or million years from now, they'll still say it was so incredibly worth it. Stories about faithful saints like our brothers killed in Turkey are what we will talk about in heaven.

The Bible is clear that each of us will stand before God and account for our lives:

> For we must all appear before the judgment seat of Christ, so that each one may receive what is due for what he has done in the body, whether good or evil. (2 Cor. 5:10 ESV)

> O great and mighty God, whose name is the LORD of hosts ... rewarding each one according to his ways

and according to the fruit of his deeds. (Jer. 32:18–19
ESV)

For we will all stand before the judgment seat of God;
for it is written, "As I live, says the Lord, every knee
shall bow to me, and every tongue shall confess to
God." So then each of us will give an account of himself to God. (Rom. 14:10–12 ESV)

What will people say about your life in heaven? Will people speak
of God's work and glory through you? And even more important, how
will you answer the King when He says, "What did you do with what
I gave you?"

Daniel Webster once said, "The greatest thought that has ever
entered my mind is that one day I will have to stand before a holy God
and give an account of my life." He was right.

Now close this book. Get on your knees before our holy, loving
God. And then live the life with your friends, your family, parents,
spouse, children, neighbors, enemies, and strangers that He has created
and empowered you through the Holy Spirit to live.

May you be able to say at the end of your life, along with Paul,

I have fought the good fight, I have finished the race,
I have kept the faith. Henceforth there is laid up for
me the crown of righteousness, which the Lord, the
righteous judge, will award to me on that Day, and not
only to me but also to all who have loved his appearing.
                                        —2 Timothy 4:7–8 ESV

a lot should change in five years

Change is not only good; it is critical. If you do the same things today that you did five years ago, you need to closely examine your heart. To repent means to change. You discover areas of your life that are not under God's control, and you repent, you change. I have been so blessed by hearing stories of people who read *Crazy Love* and changed. I love this because there are too many people saying they are "convicted" or "broken" after hearing a sermon or reading a book, yet they don't actually do anything. We even celebrate walking out of church feeling guilty, as though that were the goal. Biblically, that is failure.

> But be doers of the word, and not hearers only, deceiving yourselves. (James 1:22 ESV)

Satan, the great deceiver, loves it when we read Christian books and listen to sermons as ends in themselves. If we don't actually change, we *deceive ourselves*. We are doing Satan's work for him—he doesn't need to deceive us if we're doing it to ourselves. It's repentance that makes hell furious. Repentance is the sign of true belief. So let's keep changing.

> Godly sorrow brings repentance that leads to salvation and leaves no regret, but worldly sorrow brings death. (2 Cor. 7:10).

Repent. Change. That's not to say that everyone should move or switch jobs, but it does mean that you should be radically different than you were five years ago. No one who is yielded to the Holy Spirit can remain the same (unless you're Jesus, who was perfect to begin with).

Where I've Been

I'm still alive, and I don't take that for granted. God decided to keep me on earth for another five years since writing *Crazy Love*. Life has changed drastically, and rightly so. Pursuing the biblical truths in this book led me on an unexpected adventure that I wouldn't trade for the world. I pray for the grace to stay on this path and not be enticed by the wide and easy road, which could never lead to this kind of fulfillment.

When I wrote *Crazy Love*, I lived in Simi Valley, where I was the pastor of Cornerstone Church for thirteen years. After another three years at the church, Lisa and I believed our time in Simi Valley was done and the Lord was calling us somewhere new. Our decision to move on was confusing for people because things were going well. Usually, people move because of problems, not because of a lack of them. We loved the church, our friends, our home. There was no scandal or moral failure. There was nothing we were running from, and we weren't sure what we were running to. Ultimately, we believed there were other places where we could be more effective for the gospel, and we both believed that the Lord asked us to leave. There were good elders, pastors, and churches in our city. We sensed the Lord calling us somewhere else, most likely a place with fewer resources.

Pregnant with our fifth child, we sold our house with no idea where the Lord would lead. Believing our new ministry might be in Asia, we traveled through different cities. Everywhere we went, we asked God if He wanted us to stay or move on. It was an unforgettable time. I can't describe how good it feels to walk through the slums of India with your family, hold hands in prayer, and ask God if He wants you to stay and serve Him there. You would think that being homeless and uncertain would be stressful, but this was one of the most peaceful times of my life.

After traveling through Thailand and China, living in Hong Kong made the most sense to me. So we looked around for possible living situations and even started researching schools for our kids to attend.

Then I believe the Lord spoke to me. I can't explain it. I didn't hear an audible voice. I just had a strong sense that He put certain thoughts into my mind. This doesn't happen often, and I am very careful at these times. You never want to flippantly assume you received a message from the Lord. When this happens, I first examine the Scriptures to make sure these thoughts are consistent with biblical commands and principles. Then I examine my heart to make sure that I'm not just taking my own selfish desires and telling myself they're coming from God. After prayer and examination, I believed it was the Spirit of God leading me.

I sensed that the Lord wanted me to return to the United States. I won't get into the specific tasks He had for me, but I will say that it was overwhelming. However, there's a part of me that enjoys being given tasks that require supernatural help.

So we moved back to the United States, and I am now serving with my wife and kids in the inner city of San Francisco. We spend many of our days knocking on doors or ministering to people on the streets who are homeless and defeated. Most of my time is spent making disciples rather than speaking to crowds. I am working in partnership with other pastors who want to awaken believers to their responsibility to be His witnesses and make disciples. It has been a wonderful season of life. I have overcome some of the fears I had about sharing my faith, and I have watched my family grow spiritually like never before.

I don't want to make it sound like everything has been wonderful in my life. After the unexpected success of *Crazy Love*, I found myself battling pride and discouragement. With the rise of social media, millions are now able to voice their opinions for the world to hear. As book sales increased, so did flattery and criticism. Neither produced great results in me. The flattery led to pride. The criticism led to hurt and anger. The constant barrage of voices made it difficult for me to hear the voice of God. It was only by the grace of God that I was able to fight through and maintain some measure of humility and courage.

I share about my life not because I think everyone should do what I did, but to beg you to step into whatever adventure God has for you, whatever the cost. He leads us down different paths, but none of us is led down the path we would have chosen for ourselves. For some, living by faith means remaining where you are. Leaving could actually be an effort on your part to run from God's calling. For others, remaining could be an unwillingness to go wherever He wants. We all must search the Scriptures and examine our hearts. I just want to be one more voice begging you to truly let go. Trust whatever He has for you. It will be far better than anything you can plan for yourself.

> For whoever wants to save his life will lose it, but whoever loses his life for me will find it. (Matt. 16:25)

What I've Learned

God has taught me so much over the past few years. These are some of the most meaningful lessons I learned, in no particular order.

We Are the Weird Ones

During my time in India, the commitment level of the believers there shocked me. I visited thousands of Christians who had been beaten or watched relatives murdered for their faith. At one point, I said to one of the leaders, "Every believer seems so serious about his or her commitment to Christ. Aren't there people who just profess Christ but don't really follow Him?" He answered by explaining that nominal Christianity doesn't make sense in India. Calling yourself a Christian means you lose everything. Your family and friends reject you, and you lose your home, status, and job. So why would anyone choose that unless he or she is serious about Jesus?

I witnessed that same passion during my time in mainland China. The highlight was attending a meeting with underground church members training to become missionaries. The way they prayed and gave testimony about being persecuted was convicting and encouraging. The most surprising part of our time together was when they asked me about church in America. They laughed hysterically when I told them that church for Americans tends to focus on buildings and that people will sometimes switch churches based on music, child care, preaching, or disagreements with other believers. I honestly was not trying to be funny. They laughed in disbelief at our church experiences, thinking it was ridiculous that we would call this Christianity.

Keep in mind that the population of China is over 1.3 billion, and in India it's over 1.2 billion. Meanwhile, there are around 300 million people in the United States. This means that we are a small minority. Our views of "Christianity" are peculiar to the vast majority of the world. I used to think of those "radical believers" overseas as the strange ones. Some simple math revealed to me that in actuality we are the weird ones. The majority of believers on this earth find it laughable that we could reduce the call to follow Jesus and make disciples to an invitation to sit in church service.

If You Want to Experience God, Share Your Faith

I used to think that in order to feel close to Jesus, you had to get away from people and focus on Him through prayer. I still believe that is good and important, but I've learned that there is another way to experience Him. We experience Him by stepping out in faith. As I have conquered some of my fear and embarrassment in sharing the gospel, I have seen God answer prayer like in no other period of my life. I have found that intimacy with God comes from being alone with Him, but also from clinging to Him through difficult times of ministry.

On Sundays, I gather with a hundred people. We worship for ten minutes, listen to teaching for ten minutes, pray, and then go share our faith for a couple of hours. Then we come back together to talk about what God did. It has been a rich time, and people are experiencing God like never before. This shouldn't be surprising. After all, it was in the context of going out and making disciples that Jesus promised, "And behold, I am with you always, to the end of the age" (Matt. 28:20 ESV). And He promised that the Spirit would be given to us so that we could have power to be His witnesses (Acts 1:8). It only makes sense that if we want to experience the Spirit, we must be His witnesses. When people tell me they don't feel close to God, I ask them how often they share their faith. God empowers us for His mission. If you are not living missionally, it's doubtful you will experience His power.

Courage and Humility Must Coexist

After a couple of months in Asia, I was confident that God wanted me back in the States. He gave me clarity on what He wanted me to do, but the family and I feared the move back to America. We were close to God and had so much peace during our time outside of the States. Lisa and I had a great conversation with our two oldest kids while at the airport. We each shared our fears about going back to a land of luxury and sinking back into a comfortable lifestyle. As we discussed how we could keep from becoming complacent, my wife made the most important statement: "We can't let people talk us out of things.

Sometimes God convicts, but then we let people talk us out of it. We need to stick to our convictions."

This isn't to say that we don't consider what people say. Other people can help us see that what we call faith is actually being done out of pride, greed, or laziness. God promises to oppose the proud and is not a fan of laziness. Only fools refuse to listen to counsel (Prov. 12:15), but we must consider the source. Hebrews 13:7 says, "Remember your leaders, who spoke the word of God to you. Consider the outcome of their way of life and imitate their faith." In other words, look at how this person turned out. Is he living a life of faith that resembles what you read about in Scripture? If not, don't be so quick to listen to him. The Bible warns repeatedly against false teachers. And false teachers don't identify themselves as false teachers. They look like sheep, but they're actually wolves; they look like angels of light, but they're actually messengers of Satan.

To my wife's point, there is no shortage of people living in laziness and luxury, trying to talk you out of living by faith. There is a time to resist counsel and to refute in love. I've made the mistake of equating quietness (even weakness) with humility. I would give in to the ideas of others, assuming this was a more humble posture. Only recently did it occur to me that Jesus was the most humble person on earth, and everything He did was humble. This means that when "Jesus entered the temple and drove out all who sold and bought in the temple," and "overturned the tables of the money-changers and the seats of those who sold pigeons" (Matt. 21:12 ESV), it was a humble act! It was a strong act, but He had the people's best interests and the glory of the Father in mind. It is possible to be loud and humble. And there will be times when it is wrong for us to sit quietly.

The Book of Acts Is More Than History

For years I did not have peace when I read the book of Acts. The level of unity, commitment, and power that the early church displayed was so different from my Christian experience. People tried to explain why this could not take place today. Yet the more I studied the Scriptures, the more I became convinced that it must take place today. I'm grateful that I did not back down because I am finally experiencing it. I'm sharing the gospel alongside some radical followers of Christ, and it reminds me of what I read about in Scripture. The unity we share looks like what I read about in Acts. And we have experienced God's power, leaving us with a feeling of awe similar to that which accompanied the believers in Acts (2:42–47).

Most of us have experienced the unity that takes place during mission trips. You show up as strangers and end up feeling like a family. How does that happen? When you explore, serve, and even suffer together, a bond develops. Paul loved the Philippians deeply because there was a "partnership in the gospel" (Phil. 1:5). There is something that happens when we actually partner in spreading the gospel. It's much different from "attending church" together or going on a retreat. And it is possible to experience this on a daily basis and for life to feel like an unending mission trip. Second Timothy 2:4 tells us that "no soldier gets entangled in civilian pursuits" (ESV). Too many people spend their days entangled in civilian affairs, occasionally visiting the battlefield to relieve their guilt. It's time we stop visiting the battle and start fighting relentlessly.

> Whatever happens, conduct yourselves in a manner
> worthy of the gospel of Christ. Then, whether I come

and see you or only hear about you in my absence, I
will know that you stand firm in one spirit, contend-
ing as one man for the faith of the gospel without
being frightened in any way by those who oppose
you. This is a sign to them that they will be destroyed,
but that you will be saved—and that by God. (Phil.
1:27–28)

That describes the army God wants. He challenges us to be
fearlessly united for the advancement of the gospel. Yet churches
are filled with fear and strife. Most of us don't enjoy the rejection
that often comes with sharing the gospel. It's terrifying. We know
that it makes no sense to be quiet when people we love are going to
hell, but our fear keeps us silent. This is one reason we need each
other. We rarely "feel" like telling people about Jesus, so we gather
in order to "stir up one another to love and good works" (Heb.
10:24 ESV). We need to voice our fears so others can pray for our
courage and stir us up. When was the last time you had a group of
believers lay hands on you and pray for your courage? You might be
surprised at the results.

Paul had to remind Timothy that he needed God's power in order
to be bold and suffer for the spread of the gospel (2 Tim. 1:7–8). Peter
and John prayed with other believers because they wanted greater courage (Acts 4:29). Even Paul asked the Ephesians to pray for his courage
(Eph. 6:19–20). It is foolish for us not to voice our fears and confess
the resulting lack of peace. It has been life changing to have others pray
for my courage on a regular basis. My life is making more and more
sense in light of what I believe.

Finally, Trust Jesus

If there's one thought I'd like to leave you with, it's this: Trust the promises of God. I know it sounds obvious and maybe even a bit cheesy. Of course we should trust Jesus! We all assume we are doing this fairly well. But the Lord has recently shown me some of the doubt in my life. Like many of you, I have trust issues. I have been lied to so often, and I also recognize the deceit that has come out of my own mouth. It makes it difficult to trust.

Being slow to trust is not necessarily a bad thing. After all, Jesus was not quick to trust everyone: "But Jesus would not entrust himself to them, for he knew all men" (John 2:24). But it gets dangerous when our pattern of distrust spills over into our relationship with God. This is one area where I saw sin creep into my life.

I have become guarded. When people make promises, I assume they will not follow through. This way I can't be let down. It's much better than getting my hopes up and then being disappointed. This is a pattern in my life: Expect the worst so I can't be hurt. Many live this way. I'm not sure this is entirely wrong. But I am sure that it's wrong when this distrust is applied to God. We read His promises, but we don't want to get our hopes up. Not only is this wrong, but it robs us from the joy He wants for us. Romans 12:12 tells us to "rejoice in hope" (ESV). There is no reason to be guarded in our rejoicing. God can be trusted. He is not like everyone else.

> Know therefore that the LORD your God is God; he
> is the faithful God, keeping his covenant of love to a
> thousand generations of those who love him and keep
> his commands. (Deut. 7:9)

God will never break a promise. It is not possible because faithful is what He is. The dishonesty in all of our lives keeps us from trusting other people and even ourselves. But dishonesty does not apply to God.

> If we are faithless, he remains faithful—for he cannot
> deny himself. (2 Tim. 2:13 ESV)

God wants you to celebrate His promises without any insecurity or inhibition. His promise of forgiveness is rooted in His faithfulness. Enjoy your righteousness in Him!

> If we confess our sins, he is *faithful* and just and will
> forgive us our sins and purify us from all unrighteous-
> ness. (1 John 1:9)

Finally, rest in His promise of your future. As you read this passage, let your guard down. Don't allow Satan to plant any doubt in your mind. Celebrate and even scream in worship. Your faith in His faithfulness will give you the strength to endure whatever is necessary. Celebrate our future together:

> Then I saw a new heaven and a new earth, for the
> first heaven and the first earth had passed away, and
> there was no longer any sea. I saw the Holy City, the
> new Jerusalem, coming down out of heaven from
> God, prepared as a bride beautifully dressed for her
> husband. And I heard a loud voice from the throne
> saying, "Now the dwelling of God is with men, and

he will live with them. They will be his people, and God himself will be with them and be their God. He will wipe every tear from their eyes. There will be no more death or mourning or crying or pain, for the old order of things has passed away."

He who was seated on the throne said, "I am making everything new!" Then he said, "Write this down, for these words are trustworthy and true." (Rev. 21:1–5)

NOTES

1. R. C. Sproul, *The Holiness of God* (Carol Stream, IL: Tyndale House, 2000), 68.

2. A. W. Tozer, *The Knowledge of the Holy* (San Francisco: HarperSanFrancisco, 1992), 1.

3. Frederick Buechner, *The Hungering Dark* (New York: HarperOne, 1985), 72.

4. Wikipedia, s.v. "world population," http://en.wikipedia.org/wiki/world_population.

5. Frederic D. Huntington, *Forum* magazine, 1890.

6. David Goetz, *Death by Suburb* (New York: HarperOne, 2007), 9.

7. Robert Murray M'Cheyne, as quoted in John Piper, *Don't Waste Your Life* (Wheaton, IL: Crossway, 2003), 105.

8. Mark Buchanan, *The Rest of God* (Nashville: Thomas Nelson Publishers, 2007), 158.

9. Henri Nouwen, *With Open Hands* (Notre Dame, IN: Ave Maria Press, 2006), 65.

10. A. W. Tozer, The *Pursuit of God* (Camp Hill, PA: WingSpread, 2007).

11. John Piper, *God Is the Gospel* (Wheaton, IL: Crossway, 2005), 15.

12. David Livingston (speech, Cambridge University, Cambridge, England, December 4, 1857).

13. Attributed to Matthew Henry.

14. *The American Heritage Dictionary of the English Language*, 4th ed. (New York: Houghton Mifflin Company, 2004), s.v. "obsessed."

15. See www.familyresource.com.

16. See www.mossyfoot.com.

17. See www.standwithafrica.org.

18. Janet Benge, *George Mueller: Guardian of Bristol's Orphans* (Seattle: YWAM, 1999), 196.

19. See www.backtojerusalem.com.

20. Oswald Chambers, *My Utmost for His Highest*, June 13 entry.

A CONVERSATION WITH FRANCIS CHAN

Q: Tell us about the title *Crazy Love*.

A: The idea of *Crazy Love* has to do with our relationship with God. All my life I've heard people say, "God loves you." It's probably the most insane statement you could make to say that *the eternal Creator of this universe is in love with me*. There is a response that ought to take place in believers, a crazy reaction to that love. Do you really understand what God has done for you? If so, how can your response possibly be lukewarm?

Q: Many today are dissatisfied with Christianity as they have experienced it in the past. Some want to hold on to some form of

**spirituality but don't want anything to do with the church. How
is your critique different?**

A: Over the years, I've heard a lot of talk about what is wrong with
the church. The church has issues, and what I wrote in *Crazy Love*
calls us as the church to change many of the bad habits we have
developed over the years. But I don't ever want to come across as
a person who does not love the church. I don't want to do away
with the church; my goal is to look back to the church in the New
Testament and ask how we can renew and purify our churches so
they look more like God's intention for His church. I'm not trying
to reinvent the church or the Christian life. I'm not saying anything
new. I just want to see the church get back to where God wants it to
be. My purpose in writing these things is not to bash the church, but
to lovingly serve the church.

**Q: Why do you think so many Christians blame the church for
their failures?**

A: We all try to justify our actions. The easiest thing to do when we're
not living the way God wants us to is to blame someone or something else. It's not unique to the church. You see it everywhere: people
blaming their parents, their education, the government, their medical
problems, whatever, rather than looking to themselves and pursuing change through the Holy Spirit. The same thing happens in the
church. All of us who have the Holy Spirit have the potential to live a
"crazy love" type of life, but it's easier to not live it and blame someone
for that.

Q: You talk about people in the church not having a clue of what God is like. How is this possible?

A: Because we're taught so little about God, most people just want to know what God can do for them rather than desiring to know Him. When we present the gospel, we try to answer one question: How do I keep from going to hell? After that question is answered, we stop asking questions about God. With the American church being so concerned about converts, we don't take the time to present the God-centered universe to people. We don't try to dig deep into the truth of God. Our belief in God needs to involve an accurate understanding of who He is and the implications of that for our lives.

Q: Talk about the church and giving. Why do you think it's important for the American church to focus on giving?

A: I have seen God come through so many times in my personal life when I'm giving. I would give beyond what made sense to give, and God would just continue to bless. But as a pastor, I began to see that our church finances weren't characterized by the same focus on giving. It was like we didn't trust God to come through for the church if we were overly generous with the money He gave us. So we decided to apply Jesus's command to love your neighbor as yourself to the church's finances and began to give away 55 percent of the money that came in. This was a huge step of faith for our church, but I truly believe that this made our church healthier than it had ever been.

We also made a commitment to give Children's Hunger Fund $250,000 every three months. Over the summer, things got pretty lean financially, and I had no idea where that money was going to come from. As our last Sunday approached, I decided not to make a plea for people to give or even to mention that we had to raise the money in order to keep our commitment. That Sunday, we had an offering of $251,000. It was an immediate affirmation of God telling us, "This is exactly what I want you to do." It changes the mentality of a church to see God come through in impossible situations. A giving church is going to see His provision more than a stingy church.

Q: There is urgency in your message. Where does this come from?

A: For one thing, I've done a lot of funerals. For years I was doing at least one funeral just about every week. Many of these are for people younger than I am, and many of them are unexpected. Seeing the shock of their loved ones and realizing that God can take a person's life at any time gives me a sense of urgency.

My childhood also played into my urgency. My mom died giving birth to me, my stepmom died when I was nine, my dad died when I was twelve. I learned from an early age that tomorrow may never come. Every time I preach I want to make it the best message I've ever given in case I'm not here to give another one.

If you think about it, this type of urgency comes from the message itself. We don't need an excuse for urgency. Healing and redemption are available because of God's insane love and self-sacrifice on our behalf. Jesus sends us into the world to beg people to heed that message (2 Cor. 5:20). If that doesn't make us passionate, what will?

Q: You make a bold statement that "churchgoers who are 'lukewarm' are not Christians. We will not see them in heaven." How do you explain this? How does grace play into this statement?

A: I'm just trying to look at Revelation 3 objectively. God says that the lukewarm will be spit out of His mouth, which is drastically different from God embracing you and welcoming you into heaven. The lukewarm still need to be saved. Does it make any sense to say that a person whom God will spit out of His mouth like so much tepid water is going to be saved?

We have to be clear that salvation is not based on performance. But when we are saved we are given the Holy Spirit, and the fruits of His saving works in our lives are going to show up in the way we live. All through the New Testament a person's faith is shown through his actions. New Testament teachings are clear that someone who loves God and doesn't obey God is a liar, and the truth is not in him.

It's not popular to question someone's actions and salvation, and Scripture tells us to test ourselves and see if we're really in the faith. I believe 100 percent in grace. I believe that I did nothing; that I'm completely saved because of what Jesus did through the cross. By the grace of God we believe and are saved. But the Spirit does not lead people to live lukewarm lives.

Q: Talk about living "your best life later."

A: It's all about eternity. Hebrews 11 is all about martyrs who never got to see or experience the fulfillment of the promises. Scripture tells us that life does not end at death. We're supposed to be storing treasures in heaven. Why would we store up things on earth? It's an issue of faith.

We say we believe in an eternal reward, but our actions show that we don't. If our hope is in God and an eternity spent with Him, then our best life comes later, and we live now in the faithful expectation of the fulfillment of that promise. It's that simple.

Q: In one chapter you state, "Dare to imagine what it would mean for you to take the words of Jesus seriously." Give an honest answer: Do you think many Christians will take you up on this?

A: Unfortunately, we've conditioned ourselves to hear messages without responding. Sermons have become Christian entertainment. We go to church to hear a well-developed sermon and a convicting thought. We've trained ourselves to believe that if we're convicted, our job is done. If you're just hearing the Word and not actually doing something with it, you're deceiving yourself.

I remember preaching on Luke 6, and I brought up the passage that says, "Do good to those who hate you." I told the congregation to think of someone who hated them, and I asked, "Are you willing to go do something good for them? Will you do that? Yes or no?" I said, "Tell God right now, 'No, I will not do that.'" We're not willing to make that statement because we don't want to say that to God, but we're doing that every day. Passive disobedience is not as different from active disobedience as we sometimes think.

I'm sure that many people will read over those words and not respond because we've developed a habit of listening to the Word of God and not obeying it. But I also know that there are people out there who are convicted by the Spirit and want nothing more than to please God in everything.

Q: What do you tell people who say that you are taking the Bible too literally?

A: If someone told me that I took the Bible too literally, I would just ask them to examine their heart in asking that. I would ask them if they really believed that we're not supposed to take it that literally, or if they're just following the influence of other people who say we're not supposed to. I like to get people to think for themselves and not just go with the flow. I really believe that *Crazy Love* appeals to thoughts that all Christians have had when they're alone with God, and they realize that they are supposed to take Scripture literally. The other Christians in our lives should be pushing us to take the Bible more seriously, but unfortunately, they are often the very people who are encouraging us to relax and take it with a grain of salt.

Q: How does the American dream play into a lukewarm faith?

A: In Luke 12, Jesus tells the parable of the rich fool. This guy is successful and has an abundance of crops. He builds bigger barns so that he can store it up. He says, "[I] have plenty of good things laid up for many years. Take life easy; eat, drink, and be merry" (v. 19). Basically, he'll retire and enjoy himself: the American dream. God says, "You fool! This very night your life will be demanded from you" (v. 20).

We shouldn't worry about our lives, what we'll eat, buy, or wear. God says the American dream is absolute foolishness. Yet this bankrupt dream is being passionately pursued and defended by so many Christians! God could take your life at any time. Don't conform to the patterns of this world.

Q: Are you really advocating that we all live like religious fanatics?

A: The kind of life that I've described in *Crazy Love* shouldn't seem crazy to us. It should be the only thing that makes sense. Giving up everything and sacrificing everything we can for the afterlife is logical. "Crazy" is living a safe life and storing up things while trying to enjoy your time on earth, knowing that any millisecond God could take your life. To me, that is crazy. The crazy ones are the ones who live life like there is no God. To me that is insanity.

ABOUT THE COAUTHOR

Danae Yankoski graduated from Westmont College, where she studied English Literature and met her best friend, now husband, Mike. She published her first book at age sixteen, and has since been part of several writing projects. Some of Danae's favorite aspects of life include steaming mugs of tea; hiking, running, and being outside; thought-provoking conversations; interacting with different cultures; and playing with her new black Lab puppy, Elliott. She and Mike recently spent several months living in African and South American communities affected by a lack of clean water. Their heart is to write about these experiences in a way that moves readers beyond statistics, to truly loving their neighbors as themselves.

FRANCIS CHAN

with Danae Yankoski

To Rachel,
My daughter and friend:

You have no idea how happy I am to see the Spirit alive in you.
Let's follow Him together, forever.

CONTENTS

ACKNOWLEDGMENTS

Lisa and the kids—for supporting me as I seek to take our family wherever the Spirit leads. I know it's not always easy.

The elders of Cornerstone Church—for your patient and Spirit-led instruction in my life. I love serving alongside you.

Danae—Once again, I wouldn't have been able to do this without you. Your gift is obvious, and I admire your commitment to true, biblical Christianity.

Don and Jenni at D.C. Jacobson & Associates—for your guidance.

The team at David C. Cook—for all your work.

Jim—for designing such a cool cover. Everyone should buy a Web site from www.CloverSites.com. (You owe me a lot of sushi for that advertisement.)

Jesse and Reesh, Keith and Kristi, Gene and Sandra, Chris and Julie, Jim and Sherry, Ted and Sandy, Frank and Christy, Adam and Steph, Bill and Kathleen, Brice and Shelene, Mark and Jen, Doug and Frani, Kevin, Paul, Rochelle, and Susan. You guys didn't really help with anything, but you're good friends, and it's always fun to see your name in print.

INTRODUCTION

You might think that calling the Holy Spirit the "forgotten God" is a bit extreme. Maybe you agree that the church has focused too much attention elsewhere but feel it is an exaggeration to say we have *forgotten* about the Spirit. I don't think so.

From my perspective, the Holy Spirit is tragically neglected and, for all practical purposes, forgotten. While no evangelical would deny His existence, I'm willing to bet there are millions of churchgoers across America who cannot confidently say they have experienced His presence or action in their lives over the past year. And many of them do not believe they can.

The benchmark of success in church services has become more about attendance than the movement of the Holy Spirit. The "entertainment" model of church was largely adopted in the 1980s and '90s, and while it alleviated some of our boredom for a couple of hours a week, it filled our churches with self-focused consumers rather than self-sacrificing servants attuned to the Holy Spirit.

Perhaps we're too familiar and comfortable with the current state of the church to feel the weight of the problem. But what if you grew up on a desert island with nothing but the Bible to read? Imagine being rescued after twenty years and then attending a typical evangelical church. Chances are you'd be shocked (for a whole lot of reasons, but that is another story). Having read the Scriptures outside the context of contemporary church culture, you would be convinced that the Holy Spirit is as essential to a believer's existence as air is to staying alive. You would know that the Spirit led the first Christians to do unexplainable things, to live lives that didn't make sense to the culture around them, and ultimately to spread the story of God's grace around the world.

There is a big gap between what we read in Scripture about the Holy Spirit and how most believers and churches operate today. In many modern churches, you would be stunned by the apparent absence of the Spirit in any manifest way. And this, I believe, is the crux of the problem.

If I were Satan and my ultimate goal was to thwart God's kingdom and purposes, one of my main strategies would be to get churchgoers to ignore the Holy Spirit. The degree to which this has happened (and I would argue that it is a prolific disease in the body of Christ) is directly connected to the dissatisfaction most of us feel with and in the church. We understand something very important is missing. The feeling is so strong that some have run away from the church and God's Word completely.

I believe that this missing *something* is actually a missing *Someone*—namely, the Holy Spirit. Without Him, people operate in their own strength and only accomplish human-size results. The world is not moved by love or actions that are of human creation. And the church is not empowered to live differently from any other gathering of people without the Holy Spirit. But when believers live in the power of the Spirit, the evidence in their lives is supernatural. The church cannot help but be different, and the world cannot help but notice.

⁓⁓⁓

As I wrote this book, the question that kept burning in my mind was how can any human being write well on the sacred topic of the Holy Spirit of God? No subject intimidates me more, yet I can't think of anything more essential for God's church everywhere, and especially in the western hemisphere where it seems that the Holy Spirit is all but missing from most of our churches. I am most definitely writing from a western context, and I know that the body of Christ is vibrant and growing and the Holy Spirit active on continents like Africa, South America, and Asia. I also know that God works uniquely in various places and times, and I do think this explains part of the difference between here and there. However, I also believe that the Spirit is more obviously active in places where people are desperate for Him, humbled before Him, and not distracted by their pursuit of wealth or comforts (like we are).

The light of the American church is flickering and nearly extinguished, having largely sold out to the kingdoms and values of this world. While most people see that there is a problem, few do anything about it, and most of those who do, run toward the wrong solutions. Instead of speaking meaningfully and insightfully into the culture, we have capitulated and in many cases look no different from the world. I'm not sure if it is a calling or a sense of pure urgency that leads me to write this. Maybe both. The fact is, I don't have the "right" to write this book, but I believe it is a book that needs to be written, so I have written it, trusting that God will use it for His glory.

The Holy Spirit is absolutely vital to our situation today. Of course, He is always vital; but perhaps especially now. After all, if the Holy Spirit moves, nothing can stop Him. If He doesn't move, we will not produce genuine fruit—no matter how much effort or money we expend. The church becomes irrelevant when it becomes purely a human creation. We are not all we were made to be when everything in our lives and churches can be explained apart from the work and presence of the Spirit of God.

⸺⸺⸺

Perhaps it's not theology we're missing, but rather theological *integrity*. Many have the knowledge but lack the courage to admit the discrepancy between what we know and how we live. Hundreds of scholarly theological books have been written on the doctrine of the Holy Spirit, the doctrine of the Trinity, et cetera. This book is not one of those. *Obvious, neglected,* and *crucial* are the adjectives I would use to describe the truths I will present.

In the following chapters, I will explore the fundamental knowledge most of us have about the Holy Spirit. We will delve into some key Scriptures about the Holy Spirit and look at our own abuses, misconceptions, and even fears of Him. By journeying honestly, I hope we can go beyond our current understanding of the Holy Spirit and begin to commune openly ... that our experience with Him would be day by day, even moment by moment. That by keeping in step with the Spirit, we might regularly fellowship over what He's *doing* rather than what He *did* months or years ago. We'll be reminded of the strength and wisdom available to us in the Spirit and earnestly pray for more. As we trust in the promises of the Spirit, we will be led away from discouragement and into lives marked by confidence, power in the midst of our weakness, and the fruit of the Spirit.

My prayer is that your changed life would produce this kind of astonishment: "Now when they saw the boldness of Peter and John, and perceived that they were uneducated, common men, they were *astonished*. And they recognized that they had been with Jesus" (Acts 4:13).

Reading this book probably won't be easy. No matter what religious tradition you come from, you likely carry baggage and harbor stereotypes when it comes to the Holy Spirit. It's going to require laying aside your baggage and stereotypes so you can be open to what God wants to teach you. Are you willing to do that?

Some of you hear the term *Holy Spirit* and automatically worry that I am going to get wildly charismatic on you. Others think of extreme conservatives who never acknowledge the Holy Spirit in word or deed and hope I'm not going there. There are a lot of stereotypes (some of which are true) and a lot of abuses, and they don't come from just one side of this issue.

Some people talk a lot about—even boast of—the Spirit, but their lives do not bear His fruit. Others speak of the Holy Spirit in theoretical or scholarly terms, yet do not experience Him at work. Still others ignore Him for all practical purposes and, as you might expect, rarely experience relationship or intimacy with the Spirit. And then there is that rare person who *doesn't* talk frequently about the Spirit, yet whose life is a powerful display of His presence and activity.

Some of you would like it if I said we were going to find a healthy balance between unhealthy extremes. That's not what we're going to do. When we are referring to God, balance is a huge mistake. God is not just one thing we add to the mix called life. He wants an invitation from us to permeate everything and every part of us. In the same way, seeking a "healthy balance" of the Holy Spirit assumes that there are some who have too much Holy Spirit and others who have too little. I have yet to meet *anyone* with too much Holy Spirit. Granted, I've met many who talk about Him too much, but none who are actually overfilled with His presence.

Is it possible to get enough or even too much God? Is there a point when a person can be satisfied with the amount of intimacy, knowledge, and power of God he or she experiences? I don't see how there can be, because doesn't every encounter with God only cause us to thirst for Him more?

Let me be clear. This is not a call to misinformed extremism, but an acknowledgment that as believers we can never be "done" with

God. He is infinite and we are finite; there will always be more of His character to discover, more of His love to experience, and more of His power to use for His purposes.

I can't say exactly what will happen when you admit that you can never fully know or experience enough of the Holy Spirit yet choose to seek Him regardless. I know only that when you surrender fully to the Spirit, Christ will be magnified, not you (John 16:14).

And perhaps the core issue is really about our holding back from giving ourselves to God, rather than our getting "too much" of Him. Perhaps when a person says, "I'd just like a little God, thank you very much," she or he is really saying, "I'd rather not give the parts of my life that I really care about over to God, so I'll just hold on to this, that, oh, and that, too...."

It doesn't work that way. When I read Scripture, I see the truth and necessity of a life wholly surrendered to and dependent upon the Holy Spirit.

Paul wrote to the Corinthians that his words were not "wise and persuasive" but rather a "demonstration of the Spirit's power" in order that their faith "might not rest on men's wisdom, but on God's power" (1 Cor. 2:4–5 NIV). Later in the same letter he reiterates that "the kingdom of God is not a matter of talk but of power" (4:20 NIV).

In most churches today I hear a lot of talk and the facade of human wisdom, but I don't see much of God's presence and power. Do you?

I am tired of merely talking about God. I want to see God move through me, through Cornerstone Church, and through the worldwide body of Christ. I know there's more. We all know there's more. That's why I wrote this book—to explore with you how God has called us to more, through the presence and strength of the Holy Spirit.

I refuse to live the remainder of my life where I am right now, stagnating at this point. Don't get me wrong: God has already done so much in my life, and I am grateful for it. I'm just convinced there's more. There's more of the Spirit and more of God than any of us is experiencing. I want to go there—not just intellectually, but in life, with everything that I am.

As we begin this book, may our desire to experience more of the Holy Spirit be our starting point. And may we open our hearts and lives to His presence and action more fully than we have ever done before. By the power and presence of the Holy Spirit, may we be different people when we finish from when we started.

CHAPTER I

I've Got Jesus. Why Do I Need the Spirit?

We may as well face it: the whole level of spirituality
among us is low. We have measured ourselves by ourselves
until the incentive to seek higher plateaus in the things of
the Spirit is all but gone.... [We] have imitated the world,
sought popular favor, manufactured delights to substitute
for the joy of the Lord and produced a cheap and synthetic
power to substitute for the power of the Holy Ghost.

-A. W. Tozer-

I am convinced there is a desperate need in the church for the Holy
Spirit of God to be given room to have His way. I think we can agree
that there is a problem in our churches, that something is wrong. But
I don't think we can reach an agreement on what to do about it. Most

people do not connect what is missing or wrong with a particular need for the Holy Spirit.

A while back, our lack of openness to examining ourselves—especially in the area of the Holy Spirit—really hit me. Two Jehovah's Witnesses knocked on my door and initiated conversation. I had a lot to do, so I prepared to send them on their way. But as they began their spiel, I decided to take a few minutes and engage them. I gently told them that I found their teachings about Jesus offensive because they taught that Jesus was the same person as Michael the archangel. I told them that I believe He is much more than one among many angels; that I believe He is God. My visitors replied, "No, Jesus/Michael is the *only* archangel. There are no other archangels." So I asked them to open their Bibles to Daniel 10:13, which reads, "But the prince of the Persian kingdom resisted me twenty-one days. Then Michael, *one of* the chief princes, came to help me" (NIV). I pointed out that this passage is clear: Michael is only "one of" the chief princes (or archangels).

This caught them off guard. They told me they'd never heard or read this before. Now that I had their attention, I said, "There's no way you can look me in the eyes and tell me that you sat down one day seeking to find God, read the Bible, and came to the conclusion that Jesus is the same person as Michael the archangel. No one could come to that conclusion. You only believe it because that's what you were told, and I don't want to stand here and spoon-feed you something else." With that, I challenged them to read the Bible for themselves, rather than simply accept what they've been told about it. They went away that day and said they would consider doing that.

I left that conversation feeling a bit proud of myself because I stumped them and got them to question their beliefs. Yet I couldn't help but wonder whether I was fair to them. Had *I* ever sat down with the Bible and sought after its self-evident truth? Or had I passively ingested what I heard from other people, much like my front-door visitors?

It was then that I began reading the Scriptures as though I had never read them before. I asked the Spirit to make them "living and active" to me, though I'd been reading them for years. I asked God to "penetrate" the wrong and ill-conceived notions I'd collected along the way (Heb. 4:12 NIV). It's a great exercise for those of us who have been immersed in church culture for years.

There are, of course, dangers in this, since the Bible is meant to be interpreted within the context and accountability of faithful community. Yet even with that qualification, there is still a need for those of us nestled deep within the Christian bubble to look beyond the status quo and critically assess the degree to which we are really living biblically.

Most of us assume that what we believe is right (of course we do—it is why we believe what we believe) but have never really studied for ourselves. We were simply told, "This is the way it is," and didn't question. The problem is much of what we believe is often based more on comfort or our culture's tradition than on the Bible.

I believe we need to reexamine our faith just as much as the Jehovah's Witnesses who came to my door need to reconsider theirs. Remember, the Bereans were lifted up as good examples because they questioned the things they were taught. They made sure that even the apostles' teachings were in line with what was written: "Now the Bereans were of more noble character than the Thessalonians, for they received the message with great eagerness and examined the Scriptures every day to see if what Paul said was true" (Acts 17:11 NIV).

⸻

One of the areas we desperately need to examine is how we think about and relate to the Holy Spirit. As I said previously, if you or I had never been to a church and had read only the Old and New Testaments, we would have significant expectations of the Holy Spirit in our lives.

Think about it. Upon foretelling His death, Jesus comforts the disciples by telling them that "another Counselor" is coming (John 14:16 NIV). In John 16:7 He goes so far as to say it is to their *advantage* that He leave so the Counselor can come. And in Acts 1:4–5, after His death and resurrection, He tells His disciples to stay in Jerusalem and wait for the Holy Spirit. (The disciples obey because that's what people do when someone rises from the dead and gives instructions.) Jesus' disciples had no idea what or whom they were waiting for, or what it would be like. But they were expectant and trusting because Jesus had instructed them to wait for this good gift.

Then in Acts 2, we see the fulfillment of this promise in a way that must have shocked the disciples. The Holy Spirit's power is unleashed like no one had ever seen or experienced before, and Peter shares the amazing promise that this Holy Spirit is available to anyone who believes. The Epistles tell us of the Holy Spirit's amazing power at work in us, our Spirit-enabled ability to put our sin to death through Him, and the supernatural gifts He gives us.

If we read and believed these accounts, we would expect a great deal of the Holy Spirit. He would not be a mostly forgotten member of the Godhead whom we occasionally give a nod of recognition to, which is what He has become in most American churches. We would expect our new life with the Holy Spirit to look radically different from our old life without Him.

Yet this is not the way it is for most people. We don't live this way. For some reason, we don't think we need the Holy Spirit. We don't expect the Holy Spirit to act. Or if we do, our expectations are often misguided or self-serving. Given our talent set, experience, and education, many of us are fairly capable of living rather successfully (according to the world's standards) without any strength from the Holy Spirit.

Even our church growth can happen without Him. Let's be honest: If you combine a charismatic speaker, a talented worship band, and some hip, creative events, people will attend your church. Yet this does not mean that the Holy Spirit of God is actively working and moving in the lives of the people who are coming. It simply means that you have created a space that is appealing enough to draw people in for an hour or two on Sunday.

It certainly does not mean that people walk out the doors moved to worship and in awe of God. People are more likely to describe the quality of the music or the appeal of the sermon than the One who is the reason people gather for "church" in the first place.

I think the worst part is when you get outside the church's walls and interact with believers and nonbelievers in the same sphere. Can you really tell a difference? If you didn't recognize their faces from church, would you know from their actions and lifestyle that they were followers of Jesus? Honestly, sometimes I am embarrassed by some of my "Christian" neighbors because my unbelieving neighbors seem *more* joyful, welcoming, and at peace. Why does this happen? And how is it even possible?

Romans 8:9 says, "You, however, are not in the flesh but in the Spirit, if in fact the Spirit of God dwells in you." According to this verse, if I am a believer, the Spirit of God dwells in me. Paul reiterates that truth in 1 Corinthians 6:19–20: "Do you not know that your body is a temple of the Holy Spirit, who is in you, whom you have received from God? You are not your own; you were bought at a price" (NIV). Our bodies are the Spirit's temple. Later we will delve more into what that means for us; but essentially, it's that the Holy Spirit makes His home in our bodies. We are His place of dwelling.

And this is the question I just can't get around: If it's true that the Spirit of God dwells in us and that our bodies are the Holy Spirit's temple, then shouldn't there be a huge difference between the person who has the Spirit of God living inside of him or her and the person who does not?

This may be a silly illustration, but if I told you I had an encounter with God where He entered my body and gave me a supernatural ability to play basketball, wouldn't you expect to see an amazing improvement in my jump shot, my defense, and my speed on the court? After all, this is God we're talking about. And if you saw no change in my athleticism, wouldn't you question the validity of my "encounter"?

Churchgoers all across the nation say the Holy Spirit has entered them. They claim that God has given them a supernatural ability to follow Christ, put their sin to death, and serve the church. *Christians* talk about being *born again* and say that they were *dead* but now have come *to life*. We have become hardened to those words, but they are powerful words that have significant meaning. Yet when those outside the church see no difference in our lives, they begin to question our integrity, our sanity, or even worse, our God. And can you blame them?

It reminds me of James's frustration when he writes about freshwater springs producing saltwater. You can almost hear his incredulity as he writes, "Does a spring pour forth from the same opening both fresh and salt water?" (James 3:11). What he's saying is that so-called Christians were doing something that should've been impossible—and this kind of doing the impossible is not a good thing!

He laments, "My brothers, these things ought to not be so" (James 3:10). I echo James's exhortation to those of us in the church today: My brothers and sisters who have received the Holy Spirit, we often lack love, joy, peace, patience, kindness, etc., even while many of our unbelieving friends exhibit these traits—brothers and sisters, these things ought not to be so! Just as I advised my Jehovah's Witnesses visitors, we need to begin afresh by reexamining our preconceived ideas about the Holy Spirit and what it means to be a temple of the Spirit. There is much more to God and following in the Way of Jesus than getting a bunch of talented people together to hold a church service.

When Jesus was preparing to leave this earth, He comforted His disciples, telling them not to worry but instead to trust in Him (John 14:1). Hadn't He proven Himself faithful the past years that they had journeyed together? First, He comforted them by telling them that the separation would be only temporary and that He was going to "prepare a place" for them (14:2–3 NIV). Second, He told them that He was going to be with God the Father, and that even from there He could hear their prayers (14:12–14). Finally, Jesus gave the disciples the ultimate reassurance: Another Comforter would come. Jesus said that the Father would give the disciples "another Counselor to be with [them] forever" (14:16 NIV). In this case, the Greek word *another* means another that is just like the first (as opposed to another that is of a different sort or kind). So Jesus was saying that the One who would come would be just like Him!

Have you ever thought about the significance of having "another" Counselor who is "just like" Christ? Right now, imagine what it would be like to have Christ standing beside you in the flesh, functioning as your personal Counselor. Imagine the peace that would come from knowing you would always receive perfect truth and flawless direction from Him. That sounds amazing, and none of us could deny the benefit of having Jesus here physically, guiding and enabling us every step of the way.

Yet why do we assume that this would be any better than the literal presence of the Holy Spirit? Those of us who believe in Jesus would never deny the truth that we have the Spirit of the living God, the Spirit of Him who raised Jesus from the dead, living inside of us. I'm just not convinced we've internalized this truth and enjoyed His blessings as He intends. It seems like this is mostly head knowledge to us, and that we have not owned it. It has not really made much of a difference in our lives, to the degree that if we woke up tomorrow and discovered that it is not true the Holy Spirit lives inside of us, most likely our lives wouldn't look much different.

Jesus Himself said to His disciples, "It is for your good that I am going away. Unless I go away, the Counselor will not come to you; but if I go, I will send him to you" (John 16:7 NIV). So Jesus is basically telling His disciples, "Yes, I was with you for three and a half years, but it is better that I leave you and the Holy Spirit comes to you."

When the disciples heard that two thousand years ago, I'm sure it was hard for them to grasp. How could it be better to trade a human Jesus—a man they could talk and eat and laugh with—for a Spirit they couldn't physically see? Thousands of years later, I think most of us would also choose a physical Jesus over an invisible Spirit. But what do we do with the fact that Jesus says it is better for His followers to have the Holy Spirit? Do we believe Him? If so, do our lives reflect that belief?

My hunch is that most of you reading this book have basic knowledge *about* the Holy Spirit; but when it comes to experiencing the Spirit in your life, it's a different story. Take a moment and ask yourself this question: *When was the last time I undeniably saw the Spirit at work in or around me?* If it was recently, consider taking a few minutes to reflect on what the Spirit of God did and how you saw Him at work. Thank God for His active presence in your life, and praise Him for the way He is leading you even now.

If you are having trouble recounting a time when the Spirit was at work in or around you, perhaps that is because you have been ignoring the Spirit. Perhaps it is because you have a lot of head knowledge about the Spirit, but not much of a relationship with Him.

The reality is that the early church knew less about the Holy Spirit than most of us in the church today, at least in the intellectual sense. But they came to know the Spirit intimately and powerfully as He worked in and through their lives. All throughout the New Testament, we read of the apostles whose lives were led by the Spirit and lived out by His power.

The goal of this book is not to completely explain the Spirit or to go back to the apostolic age. The goal is to learn to live faithfully today. First of all, it is impossible for us as finite humans to completely understand an infinite God. Second, many of us don't need more knowledge about the Spirit from a cerebral vantage point— what we need is experiential knowledge of His presence. And third, we can never "go back," only forward, seeking what it means to live faithfully in the time and culture where God has placed us.

So while hopefully you will learn something new about the Holy Spirit in this book, my prayer is that it will draw you into deeper communion with the Spirit and greater experience of His power and presence in your life.

Years ago, when a random thought came into my head, I decided to share it with my wife. "Have you ever wondered what caterpillars think about?" I asked.

Not surprisingly, she said, "No."

I then proceeded to tell her about the confusion I imagined a caterpillar must experience. For all its caterpillar life, it crawls around a small patch of dirt and up and down a few plants. Then one day it takes a nap. A long nap. And then, what in the world must go through its head when it wakes up to discover it can *fly?* What happened to its dirty, plump little worm body? What does it think when it sees its tiny new body and gorgeous wings?

As believers, we ought to experience this same kind of astonishment when the Holy Spirit enters our bodies. We should be stunned in disbelief over becoming a "new creation" with the Spirit living in us. As the caterpillar finds its new ability to fly, we should be thrilled over our Spirit-empowered ability to live differently and faithfully. Isn't this what the Scriptures speak of? Isn't this what we've all been longing for?

It really is an astounding truth that the Spirit of Him who raised Jesus from the dead lives in you. He lives in me. I do not know what the Spirit will do or where He'll lead me each time I invite Him to guide me. But I am tired of living in a way that looks exactly like people who do not have the Holy Spirit of God living in them. I want to consistently live with an awareness of His strength. I want to be different today from what I was yesterday as the fruit of the Spirit becomes more manifest in me.

I want to live so that I am truly submitted to the Spirit's leading on a daily basis. Christ said it is better for us that the Spirit came, and I want to live like I know that is true. I don't want to keep crawling when I have the ability to fly.

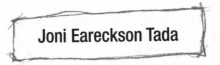

Joni Eareckson Tada

Recently I was asked, "Who is the most Spirit-filled person you know?" My response: Joni Eareckson Tada.

A 1967 diving accident left then-seventeen-year-old Joni a quadriplegic. Lying in a hospital bed, she was filled with an overwhelming desire to end her life. The thought of spending the rest of her years paralyzed from the neck down and relying on others to care for her basic needs was staggering.

But Joni did not end her life that day. Instead, she chose to surrender it to God. Little did she know that the Spirit of God would transform her into one of the godliest women ever to grace this earth. God gave her a humility and a love that enables her to look beyond her own pain and to see others' hurts. She is a person who consistently "in humility count[s] others more significant" than herself (an embodiment of Philippians 2:3).

I don't even know where to begin with all that she has done.

While undergoing two years of rehabilitation after the accident, she spent many hours learning to paint with a brush held between her teeth. Her detailed paintings and prints are now highly sought after. Her international best-selling autobiography, *Joni*, was later made into a full-length feature film. She founded Joni and Friends in 1979 to increase Christian ministry to the disabled community throughout the world. The organization led to the establishment in 2007 of the Joni and Friends International Disability Center, which currently impacts thousands of families around the globe.

Over the course of each week, more than a million people listen to her daily five-minute radio program, *Joni and Friends*. The organization she started serves hundreds of special-needs families through family retreats across the nation. Through Wheels for the World, wheelchairs are collected nationwide, refurbished by inmates in several correctional facilities, and then shipped and donated to developing nations where, whenever possible, physical therapists fit each chair to a disabled child or adult who is in need. As of 2008, Wheels for the World had cumulatively distributed 52,342 wheelchairs to 102 countries and trained hundreds of ministry and community leaders, including people with disabilities.

In 2005, Joni Eareckson Tada was appointed to the Disability Advisory Committee of the U.S. State Department. She has worked with Dr. Condoleezza Rice on programs affecting disabled persons in the State Department and around the world. Joni has appeared twice on *Larry King Live*, sharing not only her Christian testimony but a biblical perspective on right-to-life issues that affect our nation's disabled population. And on top of all that, Joni has written more than thirty-five books.

Yet it is not because of these accomplishments that I consider her the most Spirit-filled person I know. Actually, it has nothing to do with all she's accomplished. It has to do with the fact that you can't spend ten minutes with Joni before she breaks out in song, quotes Scripture, or shares a touching and timely word of encouragement. I have never seen the fruit of the Spirit more obviously displayed in a person's life as when I am with Joni. I can't seem to have a conversation with Joni without shedding tears. It's because Joni is a person whose life, at every level, gives evidence of the Spirit's work in and through her.[1]

CHAPTER 2

What Are You Afraid Of?

*The Lord challenges us to suffer persecutions and to confess
him. He wants those who belong to him to be brave and
fearless. He himself shows how weakness of the flesh is
overcome by courage of the Spirit. This is the testimony
of the apostles and in particular of the representative,
administrating Spirit. A Christian is fearless.*

-Tertullian-

Fear of rejection has paralyzed me more than once. God has answered
my prayers for greater boldness, but I would be dishonest if I did not
admit there are still times when I worry about how others view me.
Even as I write this book, I wonder how friends will respond and
how I will be labeled or even misunderstood.

Maybe caring too much about what other people think is not something you deal with personally; if so, then I am glad for it, but there is probably something else you fear. For many people, however, caring too much about what others think can be a serious, even a driving, fear.

Whole denominations have been built around specific beliefs about the Holy Spirit. I know people who have lost jobs at churches and Christian colleges because of their beliefs about the Holy Spirit. I even had a girl break up with me while I was in seminary because we believed differently about Him! It is not one of those issues that is easy to float over. This is especially true if you belong to a particular "camp" with a specific belief or bent; it is certainly natural to fear rejection from those in your camp if you change your views.

Though this fear is natural, it's not right. We are called to pattern our lives after the Way described in the Bible. We are not called to fear what following the Way of Jesus may require of us, but that doesn't mean those fears won't crop up. A life of following Christ requires relinquishing those fears when they do come. It means refusing to let your fears of what others think, your fears of rejection, keep you from pursuing the truth about the Holy Spirit and whatever else God is teaching you and calling you to.

Are you willing to pursue truth in your journey to know and be known by the Holy Spirit? Do you have enough humility to be open to the possibility that you have been wrong in your understanding of the Spirit? It's easy to get into "defensive mode," where you quickly disagree and turn to proof texts and learned arguments to defend what you've always believed. Rather than guarding your perspective, consider taking a fresh look at familiar passages to make sure you haven't missed something. You may end up with the same theology you've always had, but maybe you won't. Don't let your views be determined by a particular denomination or by what you've always been told. Within the context of relationship with other believers, seek out what God has said about His Spirit. Open up your mind and your life to the leading of the Spirit, regardless of what others may think or assume about you.

Fear has a way of channeling our thought process. Fear of stepping outside of a certain theological framework causes us to be biased in our interpretations. We work diligently to "prove" that our presuppositions were correct (another example of eisegesis) rather than simply and honestly pursuing truth.

What If God Doesn't Come Through?

Before we delve further into this conversation about the Spirit, I believe some other fears need to be identified and dealt with. One concern I've often heard (and felt) is, what if I pray for the Holy Spirit and nothing happens? What if I ask for more of the Spirit's fruit in my life and don't see any apparent "results"? It's scary to pray boldly for change or freedom from sin, because if nothing happens, then doesn't that mean God failed? Doesn't that mean His Spirit isn't all we've been told He is?

I think the fear of God failing us leads us to "cover for God." This means we ask for less, expect less, and are satisfied with less because we are afraid to ask for or expect more. We even convince ourselves that we don't *want* more—that we have all the "God" we need or could want. I can't imagine how much it pains God to see His children hold back from relationship with the Holy Spirit out of fear that He won't come through. How much it grieves Him to watch His children ignore the promises He's made throughout Scripture due to fear that those promises won't be kept! Empowering His children with the strength of the Holy Spirit is something the Father wants to do. It's not something we have to talk Him into. He genuinely wants to see us walk in His strength.

When Jesus was on earth, He said to His disciples, "If you then, who are evil, know how to give good gifts to your children, how much more will the heavenly Father give the Holy Spirit to those who ask him!" (Luke 11:13). God is a good Father who *wants* to give good gifts to His children. Sometimes I forget this truth and beg as though He needs convincing. It's as ridiculous as if my kids thought they needed to beg me to hug them. It delights my heart to hug them.

Do you believe that God in heaven gives His Spirit to those who ask? Do you *really* believe it? This truth and what it means is so incredible that no one who actually believes it could then fail to ask for the Holy Spirit.

In Acts, after Jesus has been resurrected and ascended to heaven, Peter addressed a crowd and declared, "Repent and be baptized every one of you in the name of Jesus Christ for the forgiveness of your sins, and you will receive the gift of the Holy Spirit" (2:38). We've already seen that God promises to give His Spirit to those who ask. Here we see that we receive the Holy Spirit when we begin to follow Christ.

All this leads to a question we cannot escape: Does God really give the Holy Spirit to those who ask, or was Jesus lying when He said that? I have found that it comes down to faith: Do you believe God keeps His promises or not? Do your prayers and actions give evidence of your belief?

So God has promised to give us His Spirit if we ask, if we repent and are baptized, and it comes down to whether we believe Him and act upon that promise. I realize that some of you reading this book have asked the Holy Spirit to do something and have not experienced the results you anticipated. Now you fear asking again because it would weaken your faith if God "fails to act" again. I've heard many people question God for not responding when they prayed in faith. I don't doubt that these people prayed in faith, but the question is whether they prayed for things God has promised. Often, it's the un-promised requests that God answers with a no.

There is a huge difference between believing what God has promised and praying for things you'd like to be true. I encourage you to pray confidently for what God has promised. Don't put your hope in what others promise or what you've been told you'll "get" if you are a "good Christian" (e.g., a good job, financial success, the perfect spouse, healthy children, a big house, etc.). And ultimately, you need to stake your faith in God alone, not in the gifts (good as they may be) that He gives. It really comes down to trust. Do you trust God that when He says no or "not in this way" to you, you still believe He is good and doing what is best?

Do I Even Want This?

The flip side of fearing that God won't show up is fearing that He *will*. What if God does show up but then asks you to go somewhere or do something that's uncomfortable? For many people, fearing that God will ask them to go in a difficult, undesirable direction outweighs the fear that God will ignore them.

A few years ago, I asked one of my friends if he genuinely wanted to know God's will—no matter what God desired to do through him. His answer was honest: "No, that would freak me out." He then admitted that he would rather not know everything God wants him to do. That way in the end he could say, "I had no idea You wanted me to do all of those things." I appreciate my friend's willingness to say what many secretly think and feel about total surrender to God. It's honest, more honest than most people are willing to be.

If you can relate to my friend, then at least you take God at His Word and believe the Spirit is meant to dwell in and guide our lives. When it comes down to it, many of us do not really want to be led by the Holy Spirit. Or, more fundamentally, many of us don't want to be led by anyone other than ourselves. The whole idea of giving up control (or the delusion of it) is terrifying, isn't it? Do you thrive on controlling the big and small in your life? Does the thought of letting go and listening to the Spirit's guidance scare you and only make you cling tighter to what you think you have?

The truth is that the Spirit of the living God is guaranteed to ask you to go somewhere or do something you wouldn't normally want or choose to do. The Spirit will lead you to the way of the cross, as He led Jesus to the cross, and that is definitely not a safe or pretty or comfortable place to be. The Holy Spirit of God will mold you into the person you were made to be. This often incredibly painful process strips you of selfishness, pride, and fear. For a powerful example of this, read in C. S. Lewis's book *The Voyage of the Dawn Treader* about the boy, Eustace, who becomes a dragon. In order to become a little boy again, he must undergo a tremendous amount of pain as the dragon skin is peeled away and torn from him. Only after he endures this painful process is he truly transformed from a dragon back into a boy.

Sometimes the sin we take on becomes such a part of us that it requires this same kind of ripping and tearing to free us. The Holy Spirit does not seek to hurt us, but He does seek to make us Christlike, and this can be painful.

So, if you say you want the Holy Spirit, you must first honestly ask yourself if you want to do His will. Because if you do not genuinely want to know and do His will, why should you ask for His presence at all? But if you decide you do want to know His will, there will be moments when you have to let go of the fear of what that might mean—when you have to release your grip of control on your life and decide to be led, come what may.

Is My Reputation in the Way?

I live in Southern California, where people care more about appearances than most of the rest of the United States combined. If you've lived in or even visited SoCal, you know exactly what I mean. Southern California is the land of tanning beds, plastic surgeons, designer boutiques, three-hundred-dollar jeans, nail salons, expensive real estate, excessive shopping, and hot cars. I could keep going, but I won't. It is obvious that Southern Californians care a lot about their appearances.

While this preoccupation with appearance has been taken to extremes in SoCal, it is an issue that almost every American deals with. We care a lot about what other people think of us. Maybe in Texas or Oklahoma it's about what kind of football fan you are. In Colorado, it might be how outdoorsy you seem. And maybe in New England it is which college your children attend. Obviously, these are just silly stereotypes, but the point is that we Americans tend to care about what others think of us—to an unhealthy degree. And believers certainly are not exempt from this trend.

In much the same way, many believers care too much about appearances. Even those who move past the superficial and materialistic are often very concerned with their reputation in "spiritual matters." For example, if a friend sees you reading this book about the Holy Spirit, do you worry he or she will think you too "charismatic" or "radical"? If you share about the Holy Spirit's movement in your life, do you wonder what others will think about you? Are you afraid of getting "too much" of the Holy Spirit and the possible ramifications of that? (Heaven forbid you gain a reputation for being weird or immoderate!)

Or maybe you come from a background that would consider this book too conservative. Maybe some of the biblical boundaries I've outlined are ones that people in your church label "restrictive" for a Spirit-led person.

Regardless of your background, are you willing to set it aside and just respond to biblical truth? One question I've had to ask myself repeatedly is am I even *open* to the possibility that I could be wrong in my beliefs? If so, would I have the courage to change my actions if I were shown that my interpretation of Scripture was faulty? At this point, we're all tempted to quickly respond with an "of course!" We want to believe that we are people who desire TRUTH even over relationship and acceptance. But the chances are that you care about people's opinions more than you're willing to admit.

Personally, I was raised in a very conservative church that almost totally ignored the Spirit's activity and presence in daily life. I was warned that I wouldn't feel a thing when the Holy Spirit came into me, and a hesitancy toward "taking things too far" in anything relating to the Spirit was deeply instilled in my thoughts and attitudes. After all, I didn't want to become like "them"—those people down the street who were hyped on emotions and ignored the Scriptures. I have met a lot of people with backgrounds like mine, and I've seen much damage done by choices made out of fear rather than truth. In short, we've kept the Spirit from breaking into our lives because of the fear of resembling "them."

And then there is the other side, where individuals are sometimes unwilling to listen to the warnings or checks of those "stiff and lifeless" conservatives. Perhaps you're so afraid people will think you are stifling the Holy Spirit that you won't consider examining your way of doing things—even when the Bible gives clear instructions to the contrary. Maybe you think that most conservatives are afraid of the Holy Spirit, and you fear becoming like "them."

Wherever we are at in this continuum, the point is that we need to base our understanding of and experience with the Holy Spirit on biblical truth and not on fear.

As disciples of Jesus, being in relationship with Him must be our focus. When we allow others' perceptions of us (or even our perceptions of their perceptions!) to control how we live, we are enslaved. We become entrenched in the ways of this world and do not live as citizens of heaven, which is another kind of kingdom altogether. Though there is a sense in which this kingdom of God is still future (Zech. 14:9; Acts 1:6–7), there is also a sense in which it is here now (Matt. 6:10; 12:28). As citizens of this kingdom, we are called to live in a way that reflects the reality of the kingdom of God. When we become overly concerned about our appearance, our spiritual reputation, our coolness, and our acceptance, we are living as citizens of this world rather than as ambassadors.

This is not something that just goes away. It is an ever-present struggle to maintain your true allegiance. And that is really what it comes down to: Where does your allegiance lie? Do you care about what people think when they see you, or do you care about seeking the truth concerning the Spirit of God and then living in light of the truth, holding to those promises, and enjoying that relationship?

Good Fear (or At Least Legitimate Concerns)

Having said all this, I actually think there is a legitimate kind of fear. Maybe *fear* is not the best word to describe what I am talking about. Perhaps it would be better to call it an area that we need to check ourselves in.

I am talking about quenching the Holy Spirit. As I said earlier, I think that quite often we worry a lot more about how people will respond to us than we do about how the Holy Spirit of God will respond. We think about making our friends mad or not being accepted or being thought of as different or strange. But rarely (if ever) do we consider whether our actions or lifestyle are grievous to the Spirit of the living God. When we put it that way, it seems more than a little ludicrous!

You're probably familiar with God's command in 1 Thessalonians 5:19, "Do not quench the Spirit." Are you concerned about breaking this command? Do you know what it means to quench the Spirit? For years I never gave it much thought. I didn't take the time to explore what this meant and how I could be guilty of this sin. Like most people, I just assumed I wasn't quenching the Spirit, and I moved on.

I look back now and realize I not only quenched the Spirit, but I also violated the next verse: "Do not treat prophecies with contempt" (1 Thess. 5:20 NIV). I had contempt toward anyone who claimed to have "a word from the Lord." I felt it was a righteous contempt because I'd seen people use the phrase "I have a word from the Lord" to manipulate others for personal gain. Cult leaders use the phrase to secure followers and increase their own authority. How can you disagree or even have a discussion with someone who claims they heard directly from God?

So I was against all of it. I was disturbed by any claim of prophetic speech. Looking back, I believe my concerns were valid but my actions were not. The biblical response would have been to "test everything. Hold on to the good. Avoid every kind of evil" (1 Thess. 5:21–22 NIV). Rather than rejecting the possibility of God supernaturally speaking through people, I should have tested what I was hearing in the context of faithful community.

Another valid test for prophecy is the standard of edification. The purpose of prophecy is to encourage and build up the body of Christ. Like every other gift, if it is not done out of love, it is meaningless (1 Cor. 13:2, 8; 14:3, 31). This is a good antidote to my previous inclination to ignore all prophetic speech. In doing that I was hindering the work of the Spirit, and I do not want to do so again.

On the flip side, if churches that practice prophetic utterances were quicker to reject the false prophets and prophecies by calling them out on their biblical inconsistencies ("avoiding evil"), then maybe the conservative world would be less skeptical about prophecy. If there was in place a healthy system of communal accountability and a commitment to biblical integrity, then maybe we would be slower to quench the Spirit in this regard. We would be quicker to "hold on to the good" instead of throwing out the good and the bad in one fell swoop.

Another important check is going too far with all this. No, I am not contradicting what I wrote previously. I don't mean "going too far" in the sense of getting too radical or passionate about the Holy Spirit. I mean "going too far" in the sense of stepping outside the bounds of biblical orthodoxy. I mean "going too far" in the sense of adding to the Scriptures or listening to distortions of the truth, supposedly from the Holy Spirit, and applying those to your life. This is why orthodox (as in "committed to exegetical living") and radical (as in "willing to do whatever and go wherever the Spirit leads, even if it doesn't make sense") community is vital to living lives that comply with the leading of the Holy Spirit.

Some conservatives may quench the Spirit by ignoring His working, but surely putting unbiblical words into the mouth of God is a form of quenching the Spirit as well. We need the Spirit in order to live faithfully. But we also need one another as we work out our faith.

Take some time to consider what fears you have about the Holy Spirit. It may take a while to pinpoint exactly what your attitudes and responses toward the Holy Spirit have been. Don't hide your fears. Admit them, first to yourself, and then to God (who knows all of them already yet desires to have us share our fears with Him). As you come to Him, be honest about how you fear disappointing people more than quenching His Spirit, or how you don't really trust Him to come through on His promises, or whatever else you may be feeling toward Him.

Finally, share this with people you trust, people you can have these sorts of conversations with. Allow the Spirit to continue His work of freeing you from unnecessary fear and inhibition or from unrestricted license. Surrender yourself and invite Him truly to dwell within you, whatever that may mean and wherever it may take you.

I know that by writing a book about the Holy Spirit, I will be labeled. The irony is that I don't even know how to label myself. I was saved in a Baptist church, attended a charismatic Bible study, went to a conservative seminary while working at seeker-driven churches, partnered with Pentecostal movements, and have spoken at a wide variety of denominational conferences.

I'm not even sure how to label my current church. All I know is that we definitely believe in the Holy Spirit and hope to experience more of Him every minute. When you get down to it, is there anything else we really need to know? Do we need to label one another "conservative" or "charismatic" or "radical"? What's the point in that? Let's focus on believing the promises given to us by God, on submitting to Him the fears that we have, and on surrendering ourselves fully to the work and will of God, the Holy Spirit.

Domingo and Irene Garcia

He's a mechanic. She's a hairdresser. They have been foster parents to thirty-two children and have adopted sixteen. Domingo and Irene are in their late fifties and currently have eleven children living with them, and they tell me they would take more if they could. Anyone who has children knows they could be doing this only by the Spirit's power. Imagine the amount of love, joy, peace, patience, kindness, goodness, faithfulness, gentleness, and self-control it would take to pull this off.

Domingo and Irene take the command in James 1:27 (caring for orphans) more seriously than any other Americans I know. While other people their age are figuring out how to live most comfortably, they can't stop thinking of the 500,000 kids in America who need parents. And while they see these kids as a huge blessing, they are also very open about the hardships they face daily. Perseverance has been key, especially years ago when one of their adopted sons hung himself in their closet. While their days are filled with joy, there have also been many times when they persevered by sheer obedience.

God has provided for them over and over again. One time they needed to build an addition onto their house so that they could take in more children. They didn't have the money, so Irene prayed fervently. When she looked up from praying, the first thing she saw was a sign for a contractor. She immediately asked God, "Is he the answer to my prayer?" Days later, one of the leaders in their church heard about their need and offered to build the addition for free. And you guessed it—he was the same contractor whose name Irene had seen on the sign.

One of the wonderful blessings they have enjoyed is watching their biological children follow in their footsteps. One of their sons has two biological and two adopted kids. Another son has three biological and three adopted kids. They live such extraordinary lives that CBS news ran a story on them. Even the secular world notices the unusual and supernatural love these two have shown to those in need.

For those who may think that Domingo and Irene have always been as gracious as they are today, let me share some insight from their past (I have permission). Irene has shared publicly about the early days in their marriage and the hatred she felt toward Domingo. He was abusive, and she prayed regularly that he would die. She even daydreamed about him driving off a cliff because of the pain he inflicted on her. Now she calls him the godliest man she knows.

For anyone who thinks their own life or marriage is hopeless, remember Domingo and Irene. God loves to take people in the worst of situations and transform them by His Spirit.

CHAPTER 3

Theology of the Holy Spirit 101

*What does the Spirit do? His works are ineffable in
majesty, and innumerable in quantity. How can we
even ponder what extends beyond the ages? What did
He do before creation began? How great are the graces
He showered on creation? What power will He wield
in the age to come? He existed; He pre-existed; He co-
existed with the Father and the Son before the ages.
Even if you can imagine anything beyond the ages, you
will discover that the Spirit is even further beyond.*

-St. Basil the Great-

Perhaps you wonder why I am talking about the theology of the
Holy Spirit in this chapter. Aren't the most important aspects of life

what you *do* and how you *live?* Does it really matter what you *think* about something?

These are legitimate questions.

What you do and how you live are absolutely vital. Without action and fruit, all the theology in the world has little meaning. But theology is still important—what you believe absolutely determines how you act. So while good theology at its best can lead us to live godly lives, bad theology will always point us in the wrong direction. When we study the Holy Spirit, bad theology can lead to ineffective lives or, worse yet, lives spent striving after what the Spirit of God opposes. So in this chapter we will ground our understanding of the Holy Spirit by looking at some basic biblical statements about who He is and what He does.

When I was in seminary, I discovered a lot of scholars far more intelligent than I, many of whom spent years studying particular aspects of theology. I frequently read articles by brilliant individuals who expressed opposing views on various issues, and it was hard to decide what I really believed was right. Each side would have convincing arguments and well-made points (as I said, they were brilliant). When I would finish my study of one of these issues, I typically came away with a general bent toward a particular side but could rarely say I was sure beyond the shadow of a doubt. And I never made peace with the statement one professor made: "If you're fifty-one percent sure, preach it like you're one hundred percent." How is that not deception? If I'm only 90 percent sure, why not just say so?

While some of the debates and conversations that take place are peripheral and don't have to be definitively resolved in order for us to live a faithful life, many theological issues are not this way. Some theological issues are absolutely vital to our faith. These are the ones where what we believe determines how we act.

When it comes to the doctrine of the Holy Spirit, I don't want to get caught up in abstract and nebulous distinctions. I want to focus on the theological issues that shape our faith and behavior.

As I thought about this chapter, I realized how ludicrous it would be for *anyone* to say they were going to explain the Holy Spirit. The Bible says we cannot fully understand God, and I am certainly not the exception to that rule. There are things about God that are mysterious and secret, things we will never know about Him. But there also are things revealed, and those belong to us (Deut. 29:29).

In this chapter I am going to talk about some of the things that have been revealed about the Holy Spirit. I will talk about what He does in our lives and in the world and about what He is like. Keep in mind this is not an exhaustive study of the Holy Spirit. I will not cover every verse in the Bible that references the Holy Spirit because even if I did, the Spirit is infinite and cannot be known fully by humans.

Know that even as you seek to understand the Spirit more, He is so much more and bigger than you will ever be able to grasp. This is not an excuse to stop seeking to know Him, but don't limit Him to what you can learn about Him. The point is not to completely understand God but to worship Him. Let the very fact that you *cannot* know Him fully lead you to praise Him for His infiniteness and grandeur.

As we approach this conversation, let us not forget that we tread on holy ground. The Holy Spirit brought creation to life and continues to sustain it. As we read in the book of Job, "The Spirit of God has made me; the breath of the Almighty gives me life" (33:4 NIV). I can keep writing only because He allows me to. You can keep reading only because He empowers and sustains you.

———————

I have heard the Father, Son, and Holy Spirit described like the three parts of an egg: the shell, the white stuff, and the yolk. I have also heard people say that God is like a three-leaf clover: three "arms," yet all are a part of the one clover stalk. Another popular comparison is to the three forms of H_2O (water, ice, and steam).

While these serve as cute metaphors for an unexplainable mystery, the fact is that God is not *like* an egg, a three-leaf clover, or the three forms of water. God is not *like* anything. He is incomprehensible, incomparable, and unlike any other being. He is outside our realm of existence and, thus, outside our ability to categorize Him. While analogies may be helpful in understanding certain aspects of Him, let's be careful not to think that our analogies in any way encapsulate His nature.

I love the verse in Isaiah that is typically seen as a Christmastime verse. It reads, "For to us a child is born, to us a son is given; and the government shall be upon his shoulder, and his name shall be called Wonderful Counselor, Mighty God, Everlasting Father, Prince of Peace" (9:6). Right there in that oft-quoted verse we see the Son referred to as the "Counselor" and the "Father"! This passage (and many others) keeps us from oversimplifying a divine mystery. It is not easily broken down into three main points that just make sense, but it works. And it is beautiful. The Father, the Son, and the Holy Spirit are One.

As we begin studying basic truths of the Holy Spirit, we could begin as far back as Genesis, where we see that the Spirit was present and active in creation, and then trace His actions through the whole of the Old Testament. But we will start our overview in the book of Acts, when the Spirit descended and began to indwell the disciples. The first two verses in chapter 2 say that "they were all together in one place," and that all of a sudden, a sound came from heaven that was like "a mighty rushing wind." The text says it "filled the entire house where they were sitting."

Imagine this scene with me. Jesus Christ, the one you have spent the last three years following, the one you have dedicated your life to, just ascended to heaven. You saw it with your own eyes. You and the people who have become as close as your own family are all gathered in Jerusalem in someone's house, waiting. You know that something is coming because Jesus told you about it. He said to wait, but you don't know exactly what (or in this case, who) you are waiting for. Maybe you are getting tired of wondering how many more days before something (what, you have no idea) happens.

Suddenly, a sound fills the whole house. And then tongues of fire appear and come to rest on each person present. And then it happens. Verse four reads, "And they were all filled with the Holy Spirit."

Now these are the same disciples who were dedicated to following Jesus no matter what, but who scattered as soon as Jesus was arrested.

And here they were gathered together, no doubt confused about how they should proceed now that Jesus had ascended. Yet when the Holy Spirit descended and indwelt them, a radical change occurred. From that point on, none of these disciples was ever the same. The book of Acts is a testament to this fact. We read of Stephen, the first martyr. We see Peter, a changed, courageous man. We see Paul (formerly Saul) go from killing Christ followers to becoming one and showing many others how to do so too. They were no longer timid or confused; they were bold and inspired and began to declare and live the gospel of Jesus through the power of the Holy Spirit. Think about what a huge moment this was in the lives of the disciples.

A multitude of people had gathered. Peter preached a powerful sermon, and when they heard his words, they were "cut to the heart" and asked how they should respond. Peter answered, "Repent and be baptized every one of you in the name of Jesus Christ for the forgiveness of your sins, and you will receive the gift of the Holy Spirit. For the promise is for you and for your children and for all who are far off, everyone whom the Lord our God calls to himself" (Acts 2:38–39). The text says that on that day around three thousand people became part of God's kingdom and accepted the gift of the Holy Spirit.

———————

I think it's needless for us to debate about when the Holy Spirit becomes a part of someone's life. In my own life, was it when I first prayed as a little kid and believed I was speaking to Someone? Was it in junior high, when I raised my hand after hearing an evangelist who literally scared the hell out of me? Was it when I got baptized? Was it in high school, when I actually had a personal relationship with Jesus? Could it have been in college, when I came forward at a charismatic Bible study to "receive the Spirit"? Or was it later in life, when I chose to surrender my life fully to Jesus?

We can easily fall into the trap of fixating on these questions and miss the crux of Peter's message. When I was preaching through this passage at my church, my seven-year-old daughter, Mercy, understood. She came to me afterward and said, "Dad, I want to repent of my sins and be baptized and receive the gift of the Holy Spirit." I loved the simplicity and greatness of her faith. She didn't need to debate the finer points of how and when, exactly, the Holy Spirit would come. She just wanted to obey the passage to the best of her ability. I realize Mercy doesn't have the biblical knowledge many of us do, but I wonder how many of us have the faith she has.

Is that your response to the Word? Is it clear to you that you're supposed to repent, be baptized, and receive the Holy Spirit? If so, have you done it? If not, what keeps you from doing it today?

Why do we sometimes feel that we need to debate this endlessly, running through every possible hypothetical situation and answering every theological question first? When will we simply respond to the truth we have heard and then work through our questions from there?

Now that we have a context for how the Spirit came to the first disciples and what we are told to do in response, we will shift the focus to some practical truths about who the Spirit is and what He does in our lives.

First, **the Holy Spirit is a Person.** He is not an indistinct "power" or "thing." I often hear people refer to the Spirit as an "it," as if the Spirit is a thing or force that we can control or use. This distinction may seem subtle or trivial, but it is actually a very serious misunderstanding of the Spirit and His role in our lives. In John 14:17, we read that the Spirit "dwells with you and will be in you." This calls us to relationship with the Spirit, instead of allowing us to think we can treat the Spirit as a power to be harnessed in order to accomplish our own purposes. The Holy Spirit is a Person who has personal relationships with not only believers, as we have seen, but also with the Father and the Son. We see the Spirit working in conjunction with the Father and the Son multiple times throughout the Scriptures (Matt. 28:19; 2 Cor. 13:14).

Second, **the Holy Spirit is God.** He is not a lesser or different kind of Being than God the Father or God the Son. The Spirit is God. The words *Spirit* and *God* are used interchangeably in the New Testament. In Acts we read of Peter's challenge to Ananias: "How is it that Satan has so filled your heart that you have lied to the Holy Spirit and have kept for yourself some of the money you received for the land? ... What made you think of doing such a thing? You have not lied just to human beings but to God" (5:3–4 TNIV). In these verses we see that Peter explicitly refers to the Holy Spirit as God. This is vital to remember. When we forget about the Spirit, we really are forgetting God.

Third, **the Holy Spirit is eternal and holy.** We read in the gospel of John about Jesus' promise to His disciples that the Spirit will be with them forever (14:16). And in Hebrews we read that it was through "the eternal Spirit" that Jesus "offered himself unblemished to God" (9:14 NIV). The Spirit is not just a flighty, whimsical spirit who comes and goes like the wind. He is an eternal being. The Spirit is also holy. Obviously, we commonly call Him the "Holy Spirit," and this is reinforced throughout the New Testament (Romans 1:4 and 5:5 are two examples). But consider this truly amazing fact: Because the Spirit is holy and dwells in us, our bodies are holy sanctuaries from God's vantage point. Too often we disdain our bodies as the source of sin and our fallenness; yet they are precisely where God the Spirit chooses to dwell!

Fourth, **the Holy Spirit has His own mind, and He prays for us**. Romans 8:27 says, "He who searches hearts knows what is the mind of the Spirit, because the Spirit intercedes for the saints according to the will of God." I don't know about you, but I find the thought of the Spirit of God praying for me according to the will of God extremely comforting.

So many times in life I haven't known what to pray, either for myself or for others. Other times I pray for stupid things.

For example, a while back I was out golfing with some friends and decided I really wanted to shoot in the 70s (I generally am in the 90s). So in a moment of shallowness, I prayed that God would empower me to play my best round ever. I guess the Holy Spirit was praying too, because that day I shot 115 (possibly my worst score ever). The Spirit knew I needed to work on my anger and humility, instead of adding to my pride.

In any given situation, we may not know exactly how we should pray or what we should do. But we can take confidence in the fact that the Holy Spirit knows our hearts and the will of God, and He is always interceding on our behalf.

Fifth, **the Spirit has emotions**. For a long time, whenever I read that we are not to grieve the Holy Spirit (Isa. 63:10; Eph. 4:30), I thought that was a bit of an exaggeration. It almost seems sacrilegious to say that I could grieve God. Who am I to have such power over the Spirit? That doesn't seem right. In fact, it even seemed wrong to say that God has feelings; for some reason I felt it belittled Him.

I struggled with these thoughts for a while until I finally realized where they were coming from. In our culture, having feelings or emotions is equated with weakness. This is a lie that is deeply ingrained in many of us.

God created feelings. Sure, like anything else, they can be misused and abused. But the intent and purpose of feelings came from God. Since He created emotions, why is it difficult to believe that He Himself has emotions? The Spirit is grieved when there is a breach in relationship, whether it be relationship with God or relationship with other people. When we are disunified, unloving, hateful, jealous, gossipy, etc., that is when we grieve the Spirit of God. And since He is the creator of emotions, I believe that the Spirit grieves more deeply than we can even understand.

How do you respond when you hear this? Does it bother you? When was the last time you were saddened because your sin pained the Holy Spirit?

A while back, two women from my church grew increasingly angry at each other. The three of us sat in my office, and I listened to them passionately express the reasons for their frustration. I lacked the wisdom to determine who was "more in the wrong." I just wept as they spoke. I told them I was deeply saddened because I knew how much our Father hated this. While it is rare that I'm brought to tears, there have been numerous times when I am burdened by the grief that members of Cornerstone Church have heaped upon the Holy Spirit through stubbornness and lack of forgiveness.

I believe that if we truly cared about the Holy Spirit's grief, there would be fewer fights, divorces, and splits in our churches. Maybe it's not due to a lack of belief but rather a lack of concern. I pray for the day when believers care more about the Spirit's grief than their own. In fact, I pray that some of you readers would be broken over the grief you've placed on the Holy Spirit. So broken that you actually put down this book and work to resolve any conflicts you have with other believers.

"If possible, so far as it depends on you, live peaceably with all" (Rom. 12:18).

Sixth, **the Holy Spirit has His own desires and will**. In 1 Corinthians we read that the gifts of the Spirit are "empowered by one and the same Spirit, who apportions to each one individually as he wills" (12:11). This is an important reminder of *who* is in control. Just as we don't get to choose which gifts we are given, so also we don't get to choose what God intends for us or for the church. The Spirit has a plan for our lives, for each of us. And He has a plan for the church, including your individual church body and the worldwide body of Christ.

If you are like me, you probably have a plan for your own life, for your church, and maybe even for the larger body of Christ. That's why we all desperately need to pray, as Christ did, "Not my will, but yours be done."

Seventh, **the Holy Spirit is omnipotent, omnipresent, and omniscient.** These are theological words that essentially mean that the

Spirit is all-powerful (e.g., Zech. 4:6), present everywhere (e.g., Ps. 139:7–8), and all-knowing (e.g., 1 Cor. 2:10b), respectively. These are some of His attributes that we will never fully grasp as finite human beings. In Isaiah we read, "Who can fathom the Spirit of the LORD, or instruct the LORD as his counselor?" (40:13 TNIV). Though we will never be able to perfectly articulate or completely understand these attributes, may these aspects of the Spirit lead us to praise, even with imperfect words and incomplete understanding!

—————

If the Holy Spirit dwells within you, a number of things should be a part of your life. I am going to explore several, but don't allow yourself just to read through these items like a grocery-store list. If you merely skim this list, you'll miss out on my favorite part of this book. I have benefited so much from taking each of these promises literally, meditating on them, and asking for them. Take time to dwell on each one. Consider how each one is manifest in your life; and if it isn't, spend some time asking God for that specific thing.

- The Spirit helps us speak when we are in precarious situations and need to bear witness (Mark 13:11; Luke 12:12).

- The Counselor teaches and reminds us of what we need to know and remember. He is our comforter, our advisor, our encourager, and our strength. He guides us in the way we should go (Ps. 143:10;

John 14–16; Acts 9:31; 13:2; 15:28; 1 Cor. 2:9–10; 1 John 5:6–8).

- From the Spirit we receive power to be God's witnesses to the ends of the earth. It is the Spirit who draws people to the gospel, the Spirit who equips us with the strength we need to accomplish God's purposes. The Holy Spirit not only initially draws people to God, He also draws believers closer to Jesus (Acts 1:8; Rom. 8:26; Eph. 3:16–19).

- By the power of the Spirit we put to death the misdeeds of the body. The Spirit sets us free from the sins we cannot get rid of on our own. This is a lifelong process we entered into, in partnership with the Spirit, when we first believed (e.g., Rom. 8:2).

- Through the Spirit we have received a spirit of adoption as children, which leads us into intimacy with the Father, instead of a relationship based on fear and slavery. The Spirit bears witness to us that we are His children (Rom. 8:15–16).

- The Holy Spirit convicts people of sin. He does this both before we initially enter into right relationship with God and as we journey through this life as believers (John 16:7–11; 1 Thess. 1:5).

• The Spirit brings us life and freedom. Where the Spirit is, there is freedom, not bondage or slavery. In our world that is plagued with death, this is a profound truth that points to real hope (Rom. 8:10–11; 2 Cor. 3:17).

• By the power of the Holy Spirit we abound with hope because our God is a God of hope, who fills His children with all joy and peace (Rom. 15:13).

• As members of God's kingdom community, each of us is given a manifestation of the Spirit in our lives for the purpose of the common good. We all have something to offer because of what the Spirit gives to us (1 Cor. 12:7).

• The fruit of being led by the Spirit of God includes love, joy, peace, patience, kindness, goodness, faithfulness, gentleness, and self-control. These attitudes and actions will characterize our lives as we allow ourselves to be grown and molded by the Spirit. The Spirit is our sanctifier (2 Cor. 3:18; Gal. 5:22–23).

My hope is that reading these truths about the Holy Spirit will lead you into a deeper relationship with and a greater reverence for the

Spirit—that good theology would lead you to right action, genuine love, and true worship.

Perhaps you read these verses and wonder why these things are not a part of your life. Don't be discouraged. Ask God to make you more loving or to help you put to death the deeds of the flesh or to use you to bless His children. Remember that we cannot do these things on our own, and that these are the very things the Holy Spirit does in our lives. The Father tells us to ask Him. And we can ask confidently because we are asking for things God promises us in the Bible. May we grow in relationship with the Spirit more and more, and belittle and ignore Him less and less.

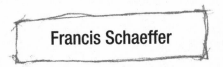

Francis Schaeffer

Francis Schaeffer was an American who was born in 1912 and died in 1984. During the course of his life he had a profound effect on Christian thought and culture. Some have even said that other than C. S. Lewis, no one helped shaped popular Christian thinking in the twentieth century more than Schaeffer did.

A onetime agnostic, Schaeffer eventually became a Presbyterian minister and an effective apologist and theologian for the faith. He recognized that Christianity and the Bible spoke to the big questions raised by philosophy, but that very little dialogue was happening between theologians and philosophers. So he began initiating such dialogue.

Francis and his wife, Edith, moved to Switzerland after World War II ended. Once there, they followed God's leading and in faith opened their home as a place where people with questions could come seeking answers. The stories of the ways they trusted God, both financially and practically, are absolutely inspiring. When they had a need, they would simply pray earnestly, often in prayer rotations through the night, until God provided.

The Schaeffers believed that Christianity speaks to every aspect of life, and this meant that honest questions were always welcome. Inasmuch as they sought God with their minds, the Schaeffers sought to live out their faith in community in a daily way. God's hand was distinctively guiding them to establish what would come to be called *L'Abri*, the French word for "shelter." It was so named by the Schaeffers because many people came there to ask honest questions about God and life's meaning in a safe place. It is still active at its original location in Switzerland, and there are several other centers around the world.

In conversations with the thousands of students and travelers who came to L'Abri (some staying a night, some months, and some years) from all kinds of backgrounds and religions, Francis always communicated that through the Bible humans can know the "true truth" about God and themselves. In addition to engaging those who came to L'Abri, Francis also wrote numerous books, lectured at universities, and spoke in several countries.

He truly loved God with all his heart and with all his mind, and thousands of lives have been (and continue to be) touched because of it. This is what happens when a person submits to the Spirit and allows Him to have *His* way in life.[2]

CHAPTER 4

Why Do You Want Him?

The Christian's life in all its aspects—intellectual and
ethical, devotional and relational, upsurging in worship
and outgoing in witness—is supernatural; only the Spirit
can initiate and sustain it. So apart from him, not only
will there be no lively believers and no lively congregations,
there will be no believers and no congregations at all.

-J. I. Packer-

My guess is that you would love to be filled with supernatural power from the Holy Spirit. You probably wouldn't be reading this book if you didn't. The question I want to ask is why?

Recently, a man dying of cancer asked the church elders to anoint him with oil and pray for his healing. Before we prayed, however, I asked the man a question I don't normally ask: "Why do you want to be healed? Why do you want to stay on this earth?" The man, as well as everyone else around, seemed a bit surprised that I would ask such a blunt question.

The reason I probed like this is because in the epistle of James, we are reminded that we often don't receive the answers to our prayers because we ask for the wrong reasons: "You ask and do not receive, because you ask wrongly, to spend it on your passions" (James 4:3). Our desire to live should be for the sake and glory of the God who put us on this earth in the first place.

So, really, why do you desire the Holy Spirit's activity in your life? Do you want to experience more of the Holy Spirit merely for your own benefit? When the answer is yes, then we are no different from Simon the magician, who tried to buy the Holy Spirit's power from the apostles. Peter's response to Simon in that situation was strong; he said, "May your silver perish with you, because you thought you could obtain the gift of God with money!" (Acts 8:20).

The Holy Spirit is not a commodity to be bought or traded according to our individual wants, whims, or even our felt needs. We absolutely cannot have this discussion about the Holy Spirit without calling our motives into question.

Right now I want you to take a break from reading and spend some time asking yourself *why* you want the Holy Spirit. Is it for power? Is it for your own betterment and purposes? Or is it because you want to experience all that God has for you? Is it because you love the church and desire to be a better servant to your sisters and brothers?

The Right Reason

While we may have our own purposes for desiring the Spirit's presence and power in our lives, so does God! First Corinthians 12 tells us that each follower of Christ is given a "manifestation of the Spirit for the *common good*" (v. 7). As we've seen, these manifestations, or gifts, are "empowered by one and the same Spirit, who apportions to each one individually as he wills" (v. 11).

So these reflections of the Spirit's presence and activity in us have nothing to do with our natural abilities, and we have not received them because we have earned or somehow deserve them. Since these gifts come according to God's will and not ours, it should be clear that they should not be used for our own boasting or entertainment.

The Spirit is intentional as He apportions these spiritual gifts to each person, according to His will and purposes. The most obvious and stated purpose of these manifestations is for the good and edification of the church. The Spirit desires to use us when our hearts are aligned with this vision, when we are filled with genuine love for the church, and when we desire to see the church grow in love for God and others.

On a scale of one to ten, how much do you love the church? As you look around at your brothers and sisters, do you think to yourself, *I love these people so much. I pray God empowers me in some way to encourage these people toward a deeper walk with Him?*

How much do you care? The Holy Spirit has given you a supernatural ability to serve the people God has placed around you. If God cares enough about His church to give you this Spirit-empowered ability, shouldn't you care enough about the church to use that gift for the same purpose?

The apostle Paul wanted desperately to go to heaven, but he was torn because he loved the church so much. His love for the church was the only thing that kept him tied to life on earth. He wrote, "I am hard pressed between the two. My desire is to depart and be with Christ, for that is far better. But to remain in the flesh is more necessary on your account. Convinced of this, I know that I will remain and continue with you all, for your progress and joy in the faith" (Phil. 1:23–25).

Do you resonate with Paul's purpose in life and love for the church? There are far too many people who seek the Spirit for the wrong reasons.

Attention

The Holy Spirit works to glorify Christ (John 16:14), yet so many who emphasize the Holy Spirit seem to draw attention to themselves. The Corinthian church was notorious for this. The church became chaotic because individuals were not concerned with the betterment of the church. They were trying to use manifestations of the Spirit for their own glory. They weren't interested in what God was doing in others; they just wanted to show off what God was doing in them. As they all fought for attention, it resulted in mass confusion as everyone tried to speak at the same time (1 Cor. 14:23–33).

A sure sign of the Holy Spirit's working is that Christ is magnified, not people. Self-glorification is something many of us struggle with. While my pride is still a struggle, God has been teaching me to see things from His perspective.

As a younger man, much of me craved God's power in my life because I wanted the attention. Now I want God's power because I don't want the attention. Jesus says in Matthew 5:16, "In the same way, let your light shine before others, so that they may see your good works and give glory to your Father who is in heaven." It is possible for us to be doing incredible things for the kingdom yet have people give glory to God rather than to us. Has this ever happened to you? Or do people praise you for your good works?

When the Holy Spirit truly moves, God is the one praised. Jesus is the one lifted up. When the Spirit moved at Pentecost, people knew there was a power present that came from God. That's why they didn't leave saying, "John is amazing! He learned a new language in a matter of seconds!" They knew it had to be God. Let's pray that God would empower us so radically that we would get no glory. That people would see our works and glorify God.

"So with yourselves, since you are eager for manifestations of the Spirit, strive to excel in building up the church" (1 Cor. 14:12).

Miracle Hunting

It is truly awesome (I try not to overuse that term, but believe it fits here) when a miracle takes place—when you experience something that couldn't happen by natural means. I have yet to meet someone who wouldn't want to see a miracle. My concern is that I've met many people whose pursuit of miracles is greater than their pursuit of God.

A lot of people want to talk about supernatural things like miracles, healing, or prophecy. But focusing inordinately on these things quickly becomes misguided. God calls us to pursue Him, not what He might do for us or even in our midst. Scripture emphasizes that we should desire fruit, that we should concern ourselves with becoming more like His Son. God wants us to seek to listen to His Spirit and to obey. The point of it all was never the miracles in and of themselves. Those came when they were unexpected, when people were faithful and focused on serving and loving others.

God wants us to trust Him to provide miracles when He sees fit. He doesn't just dole them out mechanically, as if we can put in a quarter, pray the right prayer, and out comes a miracle. Miracles are never an end in themselves; they are always a means to point to and accomplish something greater.

I'd love to witness more miracles. But when we make miracles the focus of our energy and pursuit, we ignore the priorities God tells us to pursue and we impose our own desires upon God. Sometimes we even resemble Satan, who told Jesus to jump off of the temple and perform a miracle. Of course God the Father could have saved Jesus from harm had He jumped, but Jesus refused to test His Father (Matt. 4:7) by "making" Him perform a miracle.

God does miracles when He sees fit and for His own purposes. We need to run from the temptation to conjure up miracles that

God never promised to give. Instead, we are called to focus on the priorities He has outlined for us in Scripture and ask the Holy Spirit to empower us *as He sees fit*. Ask Him to supernaturally enable you to love Him and others. And let's trust Him to display miracles for His glory, in His time, and in His way.

We also need to look for His action in the midst of our daily lives. For example, perhaps today if you live in Southern California it really is supernatural not to be materialistic.

It used to be that if I had a great worship experience, I asked God to duplicate it the next time I came to worship. Like the kid impressed by a silly magic trick, I would pray, "Do it again!" One thing I've learned about God over the years, however, is that He rarely "does it again." He's the Creator, which means that He is (among other things) creative. If we expect God to perform certain miracles or to give us a particular experience, it will be tempting to manipulate or even fake experiences of the supernatural. The point in all this is simply calling us to pursue Christ and grow in our obedience to Him, rather than pursuing the supernatural for its own sake.

Followers or Leaders?

There have been many times when I've tried to lead the Holy Spirit. I've wanted to direct Him and tell Him what to do and when to do it. The irony is that the Holy Spirit was given to direct us. Desiring the Holy Spirit means we allow the Holy Spirit to guide us. By definition, it's ridiculous to desire the Holy Spirit for our own purposes.

The Spirit is not a passive power that we can wield as we choose. The Spirit is God, a Being who requires that we submit ourselves to be led by

Him. Do you really want to be led? Even people who are natural leaders don't get to lead the Spirit. Everyone is called to be led by Him.

I honestly believe that most of us—while we might *say* we want to be led by the Spirit—are actually scared of this reality. I know I am. What would it mean? What if He asks you to give up something you're not ready to give up? What if He leads you where you don't want to go? What if he tells you to change jobs? To move? Are you willing to surrender to Him, no matter where He wants to take you? Am I?

The fact is that God is calling. The Spirit is beckoning. The real question is will you follow? Will you listen? I know I prefer a multiple-choice option for what God is asking me to do. That way, if I don't like A or B, there are always options C and D. Sometimes, of course, this is exactly how the Spirit leads us. There can be two equally good choices that God lets us choose between.

Many times, though, this is not how He works. In these cases, He calls us to do something, a particular thing, and we have the choice to obey or not. The truly startling thought is that by not submitting and totally trusting the Holy Spirit, I am not submitting to or trusting God. This is no small matter.

We all have to answer the question: *Do I want to lead or be led by the Spirit?*

⸻

Did God lead you to where you are? A lot of people in my church and in my travels tell me, "I believe that God has called me to Simi Valley." Or Wichita. Or New York. Or Greenville. Or wherever. That very well may be the case. But it could also be a cop-out because you

like where you live. You have a good job. The school district is safe
and has high ratings. Your family lives close by (or perhaps far away,
depending on your relationship with them). It makes sense that you
are "called" to be there, right?

And maybe you *are* called to where you live. But if you say you
are called to be in the place you are, a few questions need to be
considered. For example, how would you be missed if you left this
place? What would change? Basically, what difference does your
presence here make? Or, as my youth pastor once asked me, what
would your church (and the worldwide church) look like if everyone
was as committed as you are? If everyone gave and served and prayed
exactly like you, would the church be healthy and empowered? Or
would it be weak and listless?

My purpose in posing these questions is not to convince you to
"go into the ministry." I'm not about recruiting pastors or missionaries. My purpose in these questions is to get you to take 1 Corinthians
12 seriously, to believe that *you* have been given a manifestation of
the Spirit and that your church, the worldwide body of Christ, and
the world are crippled without your involvement. I write this because
I love the church and want you to trust that you are more than just
a helpful addition. You need to believe you are a vital member. As
real estate brokers, salesclerks, restaurant servers, baristas, teachers,
dietitians, therapists, students, parents, farmers, school board members, and city council officials, you are vital members of the body of
Christ. Ask yourself, *Do I believe the church needs me like a body needs
a mouth?*

FORGOTTEN GOD

As part of the Spirit's work through us for the "common good," He empowers us to be His witnesses. If you are a teacher, have you thought about how you impact the students in your classes? If you are a coach, what sort of influence do you have on your team? What about other coaches you interact with? If you are a businessperson, how do you conduct yourself toward your customers and coworkers? Do they see a person who lives according to the Way of Jesus or someone who does business according to capitalistic and self-centered standards, just like everyone else? If you are a stay-at-home mom, how are you forming your children into lovers of Jesus? How are you reaching out and ministering to the neighbors God has placed around you?

It is true that God may have called you to be exactly where you are. But it's absolutely vital to grasp that He didn't call you there so you could settle in and live out your life in comfort and superficial peace. His purposes are not random or arbitrary. If you are still alive on this planet, it's because He has something for you to do. He placed us on this earth for purposes that He orchestrated long before we were born (Eph. 2:8–10). Do you believe you exist not for your own pleasure but to help people know the love of Jesus and to come fully alive in Him? If so, then that will shape how you live your life in the place where you are.

When the Spirit Leads

When we submit to the leading and guidance of the Holy Spirit, He helps us become more holy—more like Jesus. It is a lifelong journey of putting our flesh to death, or as Paul puts it in Galatians 5, of walking by the Spirit and not gratifying the desires of the flesh. We cannot live submitted to the Spirit and at the same time gratify the flesh because these two "are opposed to each other" (Gal. 5:17). The works of the flesh are things like strife, fits of anger, dissensions, and idolatry. The works of the Spirit are things like love, self-control, joy, and faithfulness. Obviously, these are very different from each other. In making this distinction, Paul goes so far as to say that those who belong to Christ "have crucified the flesh with its passions and desires" (5:24).

The phrase *crucifying the flesh* is not exactly a friendly, appealing group of words. I think this is because God wants us to be clear on what we are getting into. He wants us to know that His gift of the Holy Spirit is really not for our own pleasure or purposes. The Spirit is meant to lead us toward holiness. The Spirit is here with us to accomplish God's purposes, not ours.

When you decide to put to death—to crucify—your flesh, you are by default choosing the way of the Spirit. You are leaving one path and joining another. The new path of walking with the Spirit will undoubtedly have its share of twists and turns. At forks in the trail, you will, at times, choose to follow the desires of your flesh, even though you left that path long ago.

The way of the Spirit is not a gentle downhill grade. Often, walking with the Spirit is an uphill trudge through all sorts of distractions and difficulties. But while the path is winding and difficult, you are constantly moving in a particular direction, and that direction is set by the leading of the Spirit. At some point along the way, you agreed with God that you were not meant to be ruled by your fleshly desires and passions (like anger, self-indulgence, immorality, etc.), and you removed the central role that these things once had in your life.

Perhaps you have not yet made this decision. Understand that it is a decision everyone must make. It cannot be done mindlessly, not when we are talking about something as intense as crucifying. Each of us has to decide whether we are going to crucify the flesh, whether we will truly walk with the Spirit. It is a choice. And it is crucial.

In addition to becoming like Christ in His holiness, being led by the Spirit will result in becoming like Christ in His love. After Paul addresses the manifestations or gifts that the Spirit gives, he writes, "I will show you a still more excellent way" (1 Cor. 12:31). It's as if he is saying, "Sure, these gifts from the Spirit are important. But let me tell you what is really important. Let me tell you about what will change the world." And in chapter 13 of that letter, he writes his famous "love chapter." In it he reminds us that without love, nothing else matters.

> If I speak in the tongues of men and of angels, but have not love, I am a noisy gong or a clanging cymbal. And if I have prophetic powers, and understand all mysteries and all knowledge, and if I have all faith, so as to remove mountains, but have not love, I am nothing. If I give away all I have, and if I deliver up my body to be burned, but have not love, I gain nothing. (13:1–3)

This passage is so powerful because Paul redirects the focus from supernatural gifts to love. He specifically says that without love, speaking "in the tongues of men and of angels" and "prophetic powers" and understanding "all mysteries and all knowledge" mean nothing.

The Holy Spirit is the one who fills believers with God's love and the one who enables us to love one another. Paul describes this beautifully in his prayer to the Ephesians:

> I pray that out of his glorious riches he may strengthen you with power *through his Spirit* in your inner being, so that Christ may dwell in your hearts through faith. And I pray that you, being *rooted and established in love*, may have power, together with all the saints, to grasp how wide and long and high and deep is the love of Christ, and to know this love that surpasses knowledge—that you may be filled to the measure of all the fullness of God. (3:16–19 NIV)

May we know this love that surpasses knowledge—the mystery of this great love—by the strengthening power of the Spirit.

Let us not become distracted from what is most important. Jesus told His disciples, "Behold, I have given you authority to tread on serpents and scorpions, and over all the power of the enemy, and nothing shall hurt you. Nevertheless, do not rejoice in this, that the spirits are subject to you, but rejoice that your names are written in heaven" (Luke 10:19–20). Our true rejoicing comes because of the grace that's been given to us.

And like our Savior, who poured out His life and blood so we have reason to rejoice, we were made to lay down our lives and give until it hurts. We are most alive when we are loving and actively giving of ourselves because we were made to do these things. It is when we live like this that the Spirit of God moves and acts in and through us in ways that on our own we are not capable of. This is our purpose for living. This is our hope. "And hope does not put us to shame, because God's love has been poured out into our hearts through the Holy Spirit who has been given to us" (Rom. 5:5).

Esther Ahn Kim

Esther Ahn Kim's biography is among the most powerful testimonies I have ever read. It was during WWII, and the Japanese occupation of Korea, that Esther's journey of faith really began. She refused to bow down at the shrines set up in every corner of her country and was eventually imprisoned for six years, from 1939 until 1945.

Knowing she was destined for prison for refusing to bow to idols, Esther spent time training herself both physically and spiritually. Each day she would find and eat food that was decaying, knowing that was what she would be served in prison. The discipline she demonstrated is humbling; how many of us would *choose* to eat rotten foods?

While preparing for prison, she memorized more than one hundred chapters of the Bible and many hymns because she knew she would not be allowed to keep her Bible. She spent countless hours seeking God through fasting and prayer. These times when she read the Scriptures led to greater clarity, and she was able to surrender her fear of being tortured.

Reading her story left me wanting more. More intimacy with Christ. More love for people. More of God in my life. And to be honest, more discipline. She was a well-disciplined believer, but there was nothing self-righteous about her. Her obedience to Christ only increased her ability to hear the voice of the Spirit, and consequently filled her with overwhelming love for the people she came in contact with.

When she eventually was taken to prison, God used her in countless way. One night a young Chinese woman convicted of killing her husband was brought in. She moaned incessantly and beat on the doors until the guards tied her hands behind her back. It was this woman that God called Esther to love and reach out to. Esther held the woman's feet at night to warm them, even though the woman was covered in her own excrement. Though food rations were small, Esther gave up her portions for three days to this woman.

Over time, the Chinese woman began to respond, carrying on conversation and eventually accepting the good news of the gospel. The woman was later executed for her crime, but she went to her death alive in Christ.

This is one of many people God used Esther to minister to. Murderers and swindlers who were utter outcasts were changed before all who watched as the love of Christ, through Esther, healed their hearts and gave them hope. Even the jailers and government officials noticed how Esther shone in that dark place. She could have just endured her suffering like a good Christian, and we would have applauded her for it. But she was not content to merely endure. She was ready every day and every moment, asking God, "Who do You want me to love for You today?"[3]

CHAPTER 5

A Real Relationship

When we are at our wits' end for an
answer, then the Holy Spirit can give us
an answer. But how can He give us an
answer when we are still well supplied
with all sorts of answers of our own?

-Karl Barth-

There's nothing worse than insecurity. So many people live in fear because they are uncertain about what comes next and their standing before God, if they even believe in God. On the flip side, there's nothing better than being absolutely sure that the most powerful Being in the universe adores you as His own child. This is precisely the confidence the Holy Spirit offers us.

Serving God and living faithfully can become a constant guilt trip of "trying harder" and "doing better next time." Maybe you can relate. I have spent much of my Christian life battling insecurity, never quite feeling sure of my salvation, living out of fear and a desperate determination to earn acceptance.

I was raised in a home where performance was everything. Unconditional love may have existed, but I never saw it. Failure was met with severe consequences. Dad was my authority; that was all there was to it. I'm not one to blame my lack of faith on circumstances, but our upbringings definitely create challenges for us. Some of you have wounds so deep that you wonder if you'll ever be able to trust. Perhaps you've subconsciously taken the failures from sinful human relationships and imposed those shortcomings onto a perfect God. Now uncertainty creeps into even your relationship with God.

It is the Holy Spirit who keeps us from this path and gives us confidence so we can enjoy intimacy with our Creator. Though I do not believe God gives us His Spirit solely for our personal benefit, it is undeniable that one of the greatest aspects of being in relationship with the Holy Spirit is the intimacy, security, and encouragement He brings us. It is then we can serve God as a beloved child rather than a stressed-out, guilt-ridden slave.

A study through Galatians helped me discover and destroy the strongholds of earning and insecurity. And it was while preaching the book of Galatians that I learned to enjoy being "known" by God.

> But now that you have come to know God, or rather
> to be known by God, how can you turn back again
> to the weak and worthless elementary principles of
> the world, whose slaves you want to be once more?
> (Gal. 4:9)

Have you ever thought about what it means to be "known"? Though I'd been telling people for years that I "knew" God, only recently have I explored the concept of being "known" by Him. It's breathtaking to picture almighty God saying, "I know Francis Chan. He's my son. I love him!" Are you confident this is what God would say if I asked Him about you? Do you know God or just know about Him? Are you acquaintances or intimate friends?

In Galatians 4, Paul explains the difference between a slave and a child. His desire was to ensure that the Galatians were enjoying the rightful privileges Christ earned for them on the cross. Many of us would say that we are children of God, but are these empty words for you? Can you say with confidence—from the depth of your being—that you know God and are known by Him?

Paul tells the Galatians that the Holy Spirit is the one who assures our hearts that we are His children: "Because you are his sons, God sent the Spirit of his Son into our hearts, the Spirit who calls out, 'Abba, Father.' So you are no longer slaves, but God's children; and since you are his children, he has made you also heirs." (4:6–7 TNIV).

These verses speak an amazing, beautiful truth! I can't fully explain it, but I've often experienced it in intimate moments with God. This is one of the precious gifts the Holy Spirit gives us. He assures us that we are in right standing with and loved by God. He guarantees believers of the gift of new life in Christ. He assures us that we have nothing to fear because we are His children and He is powerful. He tells us that we are accepted, fully and unconditionally. And He reminds us of the victory that is coming when God's kingdom is fully realized.

Paul emphasized these critical truths in his letter to the Romans:

> For you did not receive the spirit of slavery to fall back into fear, but you have received the Spirit of adoption as sons, by whom we cry, "Abba! Father!" The Spirit himself bears witness with our spirit that we are children of God, and if children, then heirs—heirs of God and fellow heirs with Christ, provided we suffer with him in order that we may also be glorified with him. (Rom. 8:15–17)

I don't know where you are as you read this. Perhaps you're tracking 100 percent and just want to voice your affirmation. If that's you, then I say, "Amen!" Maybe you are reading this and are thinking, *Well, I just don't experience that kind of intimacy with God ... the Spirit in me never cries "Abba! Father!"* If this is you, I don't have a four-step guide to connecting with the Holy Spirit. I would, however, like to suggest two potential obstacles for you to consider: comfort and volume.

Comfort (Maybe Your Life Is Too Safe)

From my own experience, I have felt closest to God when nearness to Him was a necessity. The Bible says that the Spirit comes through in situations where we would normally be afraid (Luke 12:11–12). We experience the Holy Spirit guiding us in desperate situations, such as being placed on trial for the gospel (in some countries), when we are asked why we believe in a God that allows _____ (fill in the world's most recent tragic horror) to happen, or when we receive a totally unexpected phone call that a close family member has died.

Jesus refers to the Holy Spirit as the "Helper" or "Comforter." Let me ask you a simple question: Why would we need to experience the Comforter if our lives are already comfortable? It is those who put their lives at risk and suffer for the gospel (Phil. 1:29) who will most often experience His being "with you always, even to the end of the age" (Matt. 28:20 NASB). Though this verse is true for all believers (of course God is always with us), if we are never alone or feeling like we need Him, how much do we care or need to know that God is with us?

I recently had dinner in Seoul, Korea, with an amazing man. He was one of the twenty-three missionaries who were held hostage by the Taliban in Afghanistan in July 2007. For those who don't recall the story, the Taliban executed two of the missionaries before a deal was reached with the government of South Korea and the missionaries were released.

This man told me about the horrors of being locked up in a cell, knowing that martyrdom was a strong possibility. He also shared about the amazing time they had on the last day they were all imprisoned together (their captors later divided them into groups of three and took them to remote areas). Each of the twenty-three missionaries surrendered their lives to God that night and told Him they were willing to die for His glory. There was even an argument over who would *get* to die first. One of them had a small Bible that the missionaries secretly ripped into twenty-three pieces so each could glance at Scripture when no one was watching. The Word of God and the Spirit of God got them through the forty days of imprisonment.

One of the most fascinating things this man told me was about what has happened since. Now that they have been back in Seoul for a while, several team members have asked him, "Don't you wish we were still there?" He tells me that several of them experienced a deep kind of intimacy with God in the prison cell that they haven't been able to recapture in their comfort.

This is the precious gift of intimacy the Holy Spirit offers us. It is a security that is priceless and worth any loss of safety and comfort, even imprisonment by the Taliban.

Volume (Maybe Your Life Is Too Loud)

Multitasking has become the norm. When was the last time you had an uninterrupted conversation with anyone? No phones, text messages, or to-do lists running through your mind. It's so rare nowadays to be able to look someone in the eye without interruption or distraction. A while back, I found myself talking on the phone, emailing on my laptop, and playing Wii with my daughter all at once. In my quest to accomplish much, I've lost the art of focusing on one thing or one person. This in turn has affected my prayer life, as I'm sure it has affected yours. I find it harder to simply be with God, to focus only on Him while spending intentional time with Him.

While Jesus didn't have to deal with emails, voice mails, or texts, He certainly understood what it meant to have multitudes of people pursuing Him at once. At any given moment of the day, people were looking for Jesus. Because of the priority of His relationship with His Father, He found ways to escape. He took the time to focus and be quiet (Mark 1:35). He was willing to remove Himself from people's reach in order to pray and commune with God the Father. Our lack of intimacy often is due to our refusal to unplug and shut off communication from all others so we can be alone with Him.

In the craziness of our world, it takes tremendous effort to find a quiet place. It takes time to quiet your mind and your heart before the Lord. It means turning off the music, the television, or your cell phone. It might mean going outside to your favorite spot. For some, this is curling up inside in the only place where you find privacy. For others it might mean heading to whatever wilderness is nearest to you or booking a few days at a local retreat center.

I don't know exactly what it will look like for you to be still before the Lord. But I do know that no matter what your personality, it is a spiritual discipline to be still, to listen, and to cut out the distraction and din of our world. And as we practice this stillness, this waiting, this being, it is then that we can experience deep intimacy and relationship with the Holy Spirit.

For some of you, reading this book could be a form of noise that keeps you from Him. Maybe you already hear lots of sermons and read plenty of books. What you need is direct communion with Him—to hear directly from Him and to speak directly to Him. Rather than reading my words, listen to His.

Right now I want you to take a break and open your Bible to the book of John. Read chapters 14 through 16 and give yourself some space to soak in the words you read. Notice particularly how Christ desires that His disciples have peace and how He comforts His disciples with the truth that they are not left alone. Part of His answer to how we are to have peace and be comforted is through the provision of the Holy Spirit, the other Counselor, who He promised would come once He left.

It makes sense that Jesus would say it's to our advantage to have this "other counselor." After all, Jesus merely walked beside the disciples; the Spirit would actually enter their human bodies (John 14:17). You've probably heard this truth a hundred times, but have you marveled at it? Would you be willing to take thirty seconds right now just to dwell on the fact that God is *in* you?

Astonished? This is not a distant, loose connection. This is the Spirit of God choosing you and me to be His dwelling place. That means that as I write, the Spirit of the living God is inside me. I might wake up on a particular day feeling physically tired or stressed or impatient, and humanly speaking, those things would probably define my day. But the reality is that I am indwelt by the Holy Spirit. And because of this reality, stress and tiredness and impatience don't have to define my day.

If you have received by faith the promise of the Holy Spirit, you are also His temple. As you drive your children to school. As you go to work every day. As you embark on a new, unknown season. As you go to school. As you face tragedy and pain. As you buy groceries. As you give of yourself in relationships. As you walk the dog. As you make decisions. As you live your life, the Holy Spirit is dwelling in you.

Please don't let this reality slip past you like an interesting piece of trivia that might catch your attention for a minute but that you'll never take the time to really investigate. You are a temple of the Holy Spirit. You are not just a person living your life by human power. The Spirit of God is in you; that is why Jesus said it was better for Him to go and the Spirit to come. Don't walk away from this. Delve into it and let it impact you deeply, first internally and then outwardly.

Those chapters in John, where we read of Christ's compassion for and care of His disciples, are but one small example of the meaningful relationship and deep love that motivate God's interaction with us. In Galatians 3, we read that "Christ redeemed us from the curse of the law by becoming a curse for us ... so that we might receive the promised Spirit through faith" (vv. 13–14). Wow. I am sure I have read that often enough, but until I started paying attention to the Holy Spirit, I am not sure that it really struck me. Christ redeemed us from the curse we were under *so that* we could receive the promise of the Holy Spirit. The "promised Spirit" is not a small promise. Jesus suffered a grueling death *so that* I could have the amazing gift of the Holy Spirit. How dare I take this for granted?

Because of Jesus, I have received the promise. And this Spirit is not a remote force. He takes up residence in our lives, in our very bodies, and by doing so brings with Him a deep level of security. Again and again in the Scriptures we read about being God's children, being led by His Spirit, and how we have received the Spirit of adoption.

Kristen has been a friend of the family for the past ten years. I'll never forget being with her at her mother's memorial service. As I watched her grieve, there was no doubt that she was loved by this woman who had adopted her from Korea. She was Kristen's mother, not just some lady who looked after her and paid for her food. It's been years since her death, yet Kristen still has a hard time talking about her without getting emotional. She misses Mom. This is the type of adoption God speaks of in Scripture. It's not about having an impersonal guardian who looks over you. It's about having a parent. The best parent there ever was or will be.

We have been chosen, grafted, adopted into the family of God. And now that we are a part of the family, the Spirit causes us to call out, "Abba! Father!" Remember that Abba is the most intimate form for referring to a father. It is like saying "Daddy"; it connotes a deep level of familiarity and intimacy. As God's Spirit speaks to our hearts, we can call out to God as our Abba. We will begin to experience this intimate relationship more deeply than we ever thought possible, so much so that we will begin to wonder, *Does everyone feel this loved by God?*

Don't let your personal baggage keep you from enjoying this intimacy that both your spirit and God's long for. I had issues that kept me from crying out to Abba. I often wished my testimony was like those of the drug addicts or criminals who came to know the Lord and then completely changed their lifestyles. Unlike them, I was raised in a Christian home and came to know Jesus personally in high school. After several years of walking with Him, I began to turn. I went through my sinful phase after knowing better and after having received the Holy Spirit. I quenched the conviction the Holy Spirit put in my heart over and over again.

I can totally relate to the prodigal son after he squandered his wealth (Luke 15:11–32). I resonate with the feelings he had when he was eating with the pigs, thinking he could go back to the father as a slave. Sometimes I waited a few days or even weeks before talking to Him because I wanted to have a period of proving myself. In doing this, I acted like a slave and obeyed as well as I could. I figured I could still serve Him even though I felt uncomfortable having a real conversation with Him.

Have you ever felt this way? Do you ever want to distance yourself from Him because you feel so much shame over your sin?

This was a regular pattern for me. I wanted to prove that I was sorry for what I did by being faithful for a period of time. I wanted to develop a good track record before pursuing my relationship with Him again. I wanted God to see that I could be a good servant. Then I felt good enough to talk with God again. But God didn't want a good slave who tried really hard. He wanted me to see that He was a good Father. He wants intimacy.

It takes faith to believe God is truly like the prodigal son's father, who from afar "saw him and felt compassion, and ran and embraced him and kissed him" (Luke 15:20). Lest there be any doubt, the father made it absolutely clear that his son was to be forgiven, with no questions asked. He invited his son back into his life without bitterness or requiring penance and guilt.

In the same way, the Spirit speaks truth to our hearts, such as "there is now no condemnation for those who are in Christ Jesus" (Rom. 8:1 NIV) and "[nothing] will be able to separate us from the love of God that is in Christ Jesus" (Rom. 8:39 NIV) and "He is faithful and righteous to forgive us our sins" (1 John 1:9 NASB). These are verses we could probably spout off, but often we need reminding of the power and veracity of them. And one of the Holy Spirit's roles is to do this reminding.

God said to Israel, "You will seek me and find me, when you seek me with all your heart. I will be found by you, declares the LORD" (Jer. 29:13–14). When is the last time you sought after God with *all* your heart? We are not Israel, but God still desires to be sought and found by His people. Ask the Holy Spirit to enable you to set *everything* else aside right now so that you can seek Him wholeheartedly. Tell God that you want intimacy with Him, no matter what, even if it necessitates suffering on your part. When this relationship with Him is as it should be, there is nothing more satisfying or meaningful.

Thomas and Jen Yun

Have you ever met people who are so joyful and kind you assume they are fake? After all, no one could genuinely be *that* cheerful, certainly not all the time. Thomas and Jen would be the first to admit their imperfections. But I secretly wish I could see those come out more so I would feel less guilty about myself.

Jen works in our church office, and she's one of the people I think of when I hear the term *Spirit-filled*. She doesn't have a list of accomplishments to amaze you. It is more about who she is than what she's done. I think you know the type—the person who convicts you just by how she lives her life and interacts with people.

I first met Thomas because he was a chef and co-owner of an extremely nice and expensive steak house in town. He sent a gift certificate to my wife and me so we could enjoy a meal that most pastors can't afford. While we were there, Thomas shared with me how great the restaurant was doing. It had far exceeded expectations.

In another three years he would receive back not only his initial investment but a huge bonus on top of that. The only problem was that God was calling him away from the restaurant then, not in three years.

Thomas surprised his partners by giving up the money in order to pursue the ministry God was calling him to. Thomas left the fancy restaurant and took a position at the local rescue mission. He now cooks for the homeless, recovering addicts, and others who are seeking to rebuild their lives. He uses his training in the culinary arts to teach the homeless how to cook. He then helps them find jobs as cooks at local restaurants.

Thomas and Jen are a young couple in our church body; they are a Spirit-filled and Spirit-led couple. They believe God will soon call them overseas, but until that day comes, they seek daily to follow as the Spirit leads. And they are doing it.

CHAPTER 6

Forget About His Will for Your Life!

And to expose our hearts to truth and consistently
refuse or neglect to obey the impulses it arouses
is to stymie the motions of life within us and, if
persisted in, to grieve the Holy Spirit into silence.
-A.W. Tozer-

How many times have you heard someone say, "I just wish I knew God's will for my life"? I know I've longed for this before. But now I see it as a misguided way of thinking and talking.

There are very few people in the Scriptures who received their life plan from God in advance (or even their five-year plan, for that matter!). Consider Abraham, who was told to pack up his family and all his possessions and start walking. He didn't know where he was

going. He didn't know if he would ever be back. He didn't know any
of the details we consider vital (e.g., his destination, how long the
venture would take, what the costs/rewards would be, whether he'd
receive a 401(k) or health insurance). God said to go and he went,
and that's pretty much all he knew.

I think a lot of us need to forget about *God's will for my life*. God
cares more about our response to His Spirit's leading today, in this
moment, than about what we intend to do next year. In fact, the
decisions we make next year will be profoundly affected by the degree
to which we submit to the Spirit right now, in today's decisions.

It is easy to use the phrase "God's will for my life" as an excuse
for inaction or even disobedience. It's much less demanding to think
about God's will for your future than it is to ask Him what He wants
you to do in the next ten minutes. It's safer to commit to following
Him *someday* instead of *this day*.

―――――――

To be honest, I believe part of the desire to "know God's will for my
life" is birthed in fear and results in paralysis. We are scared to make
mistakes, so we fret over figuring out God's will. We wonder what
living according to His will would actually look and feel like, and
we are scared to find out. We forget that we were never promised a
twenty-year plan of action; instead, God promises multiple times in
Scripture never to leave or forsake us.

God wants us to listen to His Spirit on a daily basis, and even
throughout the day, as difficult and stretching moments arise, and in
the midst of the mundane. My hope is that instead of searching for

"God's will for my life," each of us would learn to seek hard after "the Spirit's leading in my life today." May we learn to pray for an open and willing heart, to surrender to the Spirit's leading with that friend, child, spouse, circumstance, or decision in our lives right now.

———————

To say that we are not called to figure out "God's will for my life" does not mean God doesn't have purposes and plans for each of our lives or that He doesn't care what we do with our lives. He does. In both the Old and New Testaments He tells us that this is true. The key is that He never promises to reveal these purposes all at once, in advance.

We do know that we are called to keep in step with the Holy Spirit. In Paul's letter to the Galatians we read, "But I say, walk by the Spirit, and you will not gratify the desires of the flesh…. If we live by the Spirit, let us also walk by the Spirit" (5:16, 25).

The phrases *keeping in step with the Spirit* and *walking with the Spirit* are mostly likely familiar, but do they affect your life in a practical and meaningful way? Like I said earlier, I think dwelling on God's plan for the future often excuses us from faithful and sacrificial living now. It tends to create a safe zone of sorts, where we can sit around and have "spiritual" conversations about what God "might" have planned for our lives. Thinking, questioning, and talking can take the place of letting the Spirit affect our immediate actions in radical ways. God wants to see His children stake everything on His power and presence in their lives.

Nowhere in Scripture do I see a "balanced life with a little bit of God added in" as an ideal for us to emulate. Yet when I look at our churches, this is exactly what I see: a lot of people who have added Jesus to their lives. People who have, in a sense, asked Him to join them on *their* life journey, to follow *them* wherever *they* feel they should go, rather than following Him as we are commanded. The God of the universe is not something we can just add to our lives and keep on as we did before. The Spirit who raised Christ from the dead is not someone we can just call on when we want a little extra power in our lives. Jesus Christ did not die in order to follow *us*. He died and rose again so that we could forget everything else and follow Him to the cross, to true Life.

When people give their lives to God in exchange for a ticket out of hell, there is often no turning or change of direction, which is the definition of repentance. If all you want is a little Jesus to "spiritualize" your life, a little extra God to keep you out of hell, you are missing out on the fullness of life you were created for.

Not only this, you don't need the Holy Spirit. You don't need the Holy Spirit if you are merely seeking to live a semi-moral life and attend church regularly. You can find people of all sorts in many religions doing that quite nicely without Him. You only need the Holy Spirit's guidance and help if you truly want to follow the Way of Jesus Christ. You only need Him if you desire to "obey everything" He commanded and to teach others to do the same (Matt. 28:18–20 NIV). You only need the Holy Spirit if you have genuinely repented and believe. And you only need the Holy Spirit if you understand that you are called to share in Christ's suffering and death, as well as

His resurrection (Rom. 8:17; 2 Cor. 4:16–18; Phil. 3:10–11). Paul demonstrated this when he wrote,

> But we have this treasure in jars of clay to show that this all-surpassing power is from God and not from us. We are hard pressed on every side, but not crushed; perplexed, but not in despair; persecuted, but not abandoned; struck down, but not destroyed. We always carry around in our body the death of Jesus, so that the life of Jesus may also be revealed in our body. For we who are alive are always being given over to death for Jesus' sake, so that his life may also be revealed in our mortal body. (2 Cor. 4:7–11 NIV)

If you truly believe and have turned from the way you were headed and joined a different Way of living, then you desperately need the Holy Spirit. You know you cannot live this Way without the Spirit in you.

I think repentance is one of those words we hear a lot but maybe don't incorporate into our lives very often. When I use the word *repent*, I think about the time I was in a dating relationship, until one day a girl named Lisa came to my church as a guest soloist and caught my attention. After getting to know her, I knew she was the one I wanted to be with. I didn't consider it an option to ask Lisa if she wanted to date me *also*. I knew I had to break off the other relationship if I wanted to begin one with Lisa.

In a sense, this is what repentance is like when we meet Jesus: We totally change direction.

Some people encounter Jesus and say, "Sweet! Jesus, do You want to join the party of my life with this sin, that addiction, this destructive relationship, and we'll all just coexist together?" But repentance means saying, "Sweet Jesus, You are the best thing that has ever happened to me! I want to turn from all the sin and selfishness that rules me. I want to let it go and walk with You. Only You. You are my life now. Help me to walk away from the enslaving, worthless things in life."

Do you see the difference between these two examples? Which do you think more accurately portrays your own life? Is there anything you need to go and make right with your Savior, the One who was killed for your sake? If so, don't hesitate to shut this book and spend the necessary time. Nothing else matters more than this relationship.

So if a little bit of spirituality added in to our lives is not what God has in mind, what does He want for His children? How does He desire that we live? The fact is we were called by Jesus to give up everything. His call is to come and take up the cross (Luke 9:23).

"Taking up my cross" has become a euphemism for getting through life's typical burdens with a semi-good attitude. Yet life's typical burdens—busy schedules, bills, illness, hard decisions, paying for college tuition, losing jobs, houses not selling, and the family dog dying—are felt by everyone, whether or not they follow the Way of Jesus.

When Jesus calls us to take up our cross, He is doing much more than calling us to endure the daily, circumstantial troubles of life. The people in Jesus' day were very familiar with the cross. Having witnessed crucifixion, they understood the commitment and sacrifice of taking up a cross.

It is a call to radical faith.

Jesus is calling us to be willing to suffer anything and forsake everything for the sake of the gospel. His call is to love those who have cheated us in business; those who have spread nasty rumors about us; those who would kill us if they could; those who disagree with us politically, practically, and fundamentally. His call is to consider everything a loss for His sake. His call is for total surrender. He calls us to give up all that we have, to give even to the point of offering up our lives as a living sacrifice. His call means realizing that His power is made perfect in our weakness, that when we are weak we are also strong (2 Cor. 12:9–10).

Do you remember the story where Jesus saw people putting gifts into the offering box? At first some rich people gave, and it sounds like their contributions must have been monetarily large. Then Jesus pointed out a widow (the text even says a "poor widow") who put in two small copper coins. Notice Christ's words in response to what he witnessed: "Truly, I tell you, this poor widow has put in more than all of them. For they all contributed out of their abundance, but she out of her poverty put in all she had to live on" (Luke 21:3–4). Jesus commends this woman, whom the world—those people with power and money—overlooked and perhaps even derided. Jesus praises her for her revolutionary faith, for holding nothing back. She literally gave everything she had, even though she was a "poor widow" with no other means of income or support. And Jesus holds her up as an example.

What if you could hear the voice of the Holy Spirit and He asked you to literally give *everything* you owned? What if He asked you to sell *all* your possessions and give the money to the poor? Could you do it? Before you start explaining why He would never ask that of you, take a moment and answer the question honestly. It's not out of His character to ask for everything.

I don't know about you, but that challenges me like crazy. I say I want to give it all to God, to truly submit myself to the leading of the Holy Spirit. But I won't lie; sometimes the reality of what that means leaves me wanting to hold back a little. There are things on this earth that I *really* enjoy, like surfing, golfing, eating out, and laughing with friends. I know what you're thinking: that those things are not sinful. And you are right. But that doesn't mean the Spirit will not lead me to forgo those things occasionally or maybe even permanently for His purposes and the glory of the Father.

I struggle to always and actually keep in step with the Spirit moment by moment. To submit and give up everything truly is radical and terrifying. However, when I think deeply about it, walking in my own wisdom, contrary to the Spirit's leading, is even more frightful. Though I struggle, I know that ultimately I want nothing more than to live in total surrender and abandonment to the Spirit every moment I have left on this earth.

The Spirit may lead me into total sacrifice financially, or He may lead me toward humiliation in the opinions of people around me.

The Spirit may ask me to move to a different city, a different state, or a different country. The Spirit may ask me to stay where I am and spend my time in very different ways than I do now. He could lead me toward actions like in 2 Samuel 6, where David danced (it says in "a linen ephod," the equivalent of priestly underwear) before the Lord "with all his might" (v. 14). Others were shamed by his undignified display of worship to God, yet David said that he didn't care and that he would become even more undignified for the sake of the Lord. All he cared about was worshipping his God.

When I read this story, part of me says, "Yes, I want to live like David. I want to forget about what others think and worship my King with all of me." The other part of me says, "Okay, but practically, what does that look like?" How do I walk in such intimacy with the Spirit that my genuine response when He moves is to dance with abandon, heedless of those around me who might consider it inappropriate? And do I really need not to care about what others think of me?

The crux of it, I believe, is realizing that being filled with the Spirit is not a one-time act. As we read in Galatians about the Spirit and the flesh, walking with the Spirit implies an ongoing relationship. Being filled with the Spirit is not limited to the day we first meet Christ. Instead, throughout Scripture we read of a relationship that calls us into an active pursuit of the Spirit.

Christians can't ever lose the Spirit, but His filling is something we should constantly pursue. This business of sanctification is a lifelong process we are engaged in. Second Corinthians 3:18 says, "We all, who with unveiled faces contemplate the Lord's glory, are being transformed into his image with ever-increasing glory, which comes from the Lord, who is the Spirit" (TNIV). (See also 2 Thess. 2:13 and Rom. 15:16.)

Imagine I buy a treadmill to lose some weight. Three months later I take it back to the store and complain to the clerk that it didn't work—I didn't lose a pound. He asks me, "What was the problem? Did it not work properly?" I respond, "I don't know if it works. I never ran on it. I just know I didn't lose any weight, so I am done with it!"

This may seem like a silly example, but change the details and suddenly it sounds pretty familiar:

"I have prayed for the Holy Spirit to free me from my lust, and I am still addicted to pornography." Or, "I have prayed for years to be able to forgive my dad, but I am still racked with anger and bitterness thirty years down the road." "I have prayed for years to be free of my gluttony, but despite prayer, spiritually based support groups, and dieting, I am still a compulsive, unhealthy eater." Fill in whatever sin plagues you and suddenly the treadmill illustration doesn't seem so silly. In fact, it seems like those prayers for freedom from that ongoing sin didn't really "work" in much the same way the treadmill didn't help me lose any weight.

Receiving freedom and healing in answer to prayer is generally not something that is done to you, a situation in which you are just a passive participant. Occasionally God works this way and simply heals or frees a person outright. He is certainly capable of this. But in my experience, He typically asks us to play an active role in the journey toward wholeness. He doesn't need our help but invites us to participate. Often this journey to freedom takes time, sometimes a very long time. And it takes perseverance. It takes participation on our part. We have to get on the treadmill and run—merely looking at the workout machine doesn't do a whole lot. (See also Rom. 12:11 and 1 Thess. 5:19.)

Have you been stuck in a cycle of sin for a long time? Have you given up on the Holy Spirit and resigned yourself to thinking that He doesn't "work" or doesn't have the power to bring freedom, at least not in your life? If this is you, then maybe you have not internalized the reality that walking in the Spirit requires action on your part.

Because the fact is that if you were in step with the Holy Spirit, listening to and obeying Him, you wouldn't sin (Gal. 5:16). In any given moment, it is impossible to live in the power of the Spirit and sin at the same time. Sin is wholly opposed to everything that is of the Spirit. They really are mutually exclusive and totally contrary to each other.

This does not mean that if you sin, you don't have the Holy Spirit or aren't a follower of Christ. It does mean that when you are sinning, you are not simultaneously submitted to the authority and presence of the Holy Spirit in your life. He is still present, but you are most likely suppressing or ignoring His counsel.

The hopeful part in all this is that even when we do ignore the Spirit and sin, the Holy Spirit convicts us of that sin. Though at times we sin, we are not ruled and enslaved by sin as we once were. We have cut off the headship of sin in our lives. When we are attuned to the Spirit, we are reminded of this freeing reality.

It's obvious when someone is not walking in the Spirit (at least not consistently). What you see and experience from such a person is usually along the lines of rage, selfishness, dissension, bitterness, and envy. However, when a person is habitually and actively submitted to the Spirit, what comes out of his or her life is the fruit of the Spirit. The Holy Spirit will not—*cannot*—lead you into sin. If the Holy Spirit is in you, as a believer, then when you sin you are not listening to the Spirit's leading.

Haven't you met those rare people who you can tell are daily keeping in step with the Spirit? Somehow they exude graciousness and peacefulness to a degree that is not humanly possible. Don't you want that in your own life? I mean, who really wants to be a stressed-out, angry, selfish person? It's not much fun, for you or anyone who happens to come in contact with you.

Several people in my own life come to mind when I think about people who walk with the Spirit daily. It would be easy to start comparing ourselves to others in this area. I can already hear the thought progression: *Well, I am obviously more Spirit-led than that person....*

Instead of wasting time deliberating over whether others are walking with the Spirit (which is definitely *not* our job), I challenge you to examine yourself. Look at the "fruit" of your own life and let it be a gauge for you of your own connectedness with the Spirit. Do you listen to the Holy Spirit as you stand in line at the post office? Perhaps He is asking you to begin a conversation with the elderly lady in front of you. Do you allow the Holy Spirit to lead when you are making your budget? Perhaps He will direct you to allocate the monies differently than you otherwise would. Do you submit to the Holy Spirit as you spend time with your family? Often it is family members who are most difficult to love, and we need the Spirit's help to love them well. These are just a few of the many, many areas of our lives that we can submit to the Spirit's leading. Take some time to think about areas in your own life where you tend just to do your own thing, heedless of the Spirit's will and call.

Living by the Spirit implies a habitual, continual, and active interaction with the Holy Spirit. While this sounds exhausting, it really isn't because all of this living and action is done in the power of the Spirit. It is not by your own strength.

This, however, brings up a whole other confusing issue: Is it God's work or my work? God's responsibility or mine? Paul addresses this when he writes to the Galatians. He calls them out, asking whom they had been bewitched by (quite an accusation!). He asks, "Having begun by the Spirit, are you now being perfected by the flesh?" (3:3).

I think each of us has a strong tendency to attempt to wrestle control from the Spirit and "do" this life on our own. Each of us tends to switch from living the gospel of grace to trusting in a system of works. That's why Paul brings up this issue with the churches in Galatia. He knows it's hard to truly depend on sustenance and guidance from the Spirit rather than merely on our own wisdom and effort.

Remember the treadmill illustration? Perhaps you wonder how the concept of our actions fits in with the gospel of grace, which cannot be merited or earned. Suppose I bake a loaf of bread and you asked me, "Which ingredient is more important, the yeast or the flour?" I would look at my still-warm loaf of bread and reply that both are fundamentally necessary to the making of bread; you simply would not have bread without both yeast and flour.

This illustration bears a similarity to our spiritual lives. If we never responded to God, if we never acted based on what He has done for us, there wouldn't be much of a relationship there. God is still real and moving, but at some point we have to respond and act because of what He's done. Like yeast and flour are both necessary to bread, both God's action and our response-action are necessary in this relationship with God.

In the book of Philippians, Paul writes, "Therefore, my beloved, as you have always obeyed, so now, not only as in my presence but much more in my absence, work out your own salvation with fear and trembling, for it is God who works in you, both to will and to work for his good pleasure" (2:12–13). I love the apparent contradiction in this passage. Paul says in one breath, "Work out your own salvation," and in the next, "It is God who works in you." The both-ness here doesn't allow us to escape with a simple conclusion. Yes, it is God who works in you. And, yes, there is work for you to do. Yes, the Spirit empowers you to do the work. And, yes, you do the work.

Like many things in life, there really isn't a sew-it-all-up solution. And I love that. God is big and mysterious enough that we cannot simply put a label on this process and move on. It requires continual engagement and wrestling and discovering how to live a Spirit-filled life today. Not ten years from now. Not tomorrow. But right now, in the particular time and place He has put us. As we "work out our salvation" and as "God works in us." Let us keep in step.

Dave Phillips

Years ago, Dave Phillips and his wife, Lynn, had a talk about the callings they felt God was stirring in them. As they discussed what they were most passionate about, they agreed that bringing relief to suffering children and reaching the next generation with the gospel were at the top of the list. The thought of starting a relief agency was considered, but Dave's response was, "But that would mean I have to talk in front of people." By nature, Dave is a very quiet, behind-the-scenes man.

But after much prayer, Dave set aside his fears, and he and Lynn started Children's Hunger Fund out of their garage. Six weeks after CHF was launched, in January of 1992, he received a phone call from the director of a cancer treatment center in Honduras asking if there was any way he could obtain a certain drug for seven children who would die without it. Dave wrote down the name of the drug and told the director that he had no idea how to get this type of drug. They then prayed over the phone and asked God to provide.

As Dave hung up the phone, before he even let go of the receiver, the phone rang again. It was a pharmaceutical company in New Jersey asking Dave if he would have any use for 48,000 vials of *that exact drug!* Not only did they offer him eight million dollars' worth of this drug, but they told him they would airlift it to anyplace in the world! Dave would later learn that the company was one of only two that manufactured this particular drug in the United States.

Within forty-eight hours, Dave had the drug sent to the treatment center in Honduras and to twenty other locations as well. It was then he believed firmly that God was at work, validating his calling to this ministry.

Year after year, God continues to provide supernaturally. Today they have distributed more than $950 million in food and other relief to more than ten million kids in seventy countries and thirty-two states. Children's Hunger Fund has distributed more than 150 million pounds of food and 110 million toys.

The uniqueness of CHF is that they train and equip volunteers from local churches to distribute the food through home deliveries in the United States and other countries. Going from family to family, they find the poorest of the poor and share not only food but love and the gospel. Forbes.com consistently rates CHF at the top of their list of America's most cost-effective charities.

One of the most beautiful things about this story is that if you met Dave, you would never think he was the CEO of a major organization. He is a quiet, soft-spoken man—not the type you envision leading a movement. His power doesn't necessarily come from a natural giftedness but from a dedicated prayer life. As a close, personal friend of Dave's, I don't know that I've ever spent time with him without spending time in prayer.

Dave lives a life we should long for and, incredibly, the kind of life that is offered to us as well. A life in which people know that our accomplishments could not have been attained by our own power. A life that brings glory to God in heaven.[4]

CHAPTER 7

Supernatural Church

*What the soul is in our body, the Holy Spirit is
in the body of Christ, which is the church.*

-Augustine-

I bet you'd agree that a group of talented, charismatic leaders can
draw a crowd. Find the right creative team, musicians, and speakers,
and you can grow any church. It doesn't even have to be a Christian
church. The fact is that without making a conscious choice to depend
on the Holy Spirit, we can do a lot. (Although without the Spirit,
we wouldn't actually be drawing our next breath—but I am talking
about cognizant and intentional dependence on our part.) My point
is that a growing and energetic gathering is not necessarily evidence
of the Holy Spirit's work.

We all have our natural talents and bents, things that we are "gifted at" (of course, the reality is that those gifts too are ultimately from God). I have friends who are gifted artists, and I love watching them paint and draw. Those of us who are artistically challenged are stunned by the beautiful works of art they create. Others are good with people and can easily work in a variety of jobs that require people skills. Still others know how to sell things, no matter what the product is. And some have the skill set required to pull off a decent church.

A while back I asked my church during a service if they thought I could successfully sell insurance as a career. I did this because I know that some of my natural skills are connected to interacting with people and speaking. The fact is that we all have jobs that come naturally for us. Because of how I was made, I could be an insurance salesman if I had a little bit of training. And I can probably "pull off" a fairly adequate church on my own as well. But who wants or needs that?

I don't want my life to be explainable without the Holy Spirit. I want people to look at my life and know that I couldn't be doing this by my own power. I want to live in such a way that I am desperate for Him to come through. That if He doesn't come through, I am screwed. (I probably shouldn't write that word here, but it's how I truly feel about this.)

There was a time when I got excited over a crowd showing up to hear me preach, but those days are long gone. Now I deeply desire that the Spirit of God would do things that I *know* are not of me and that cannot be faked or accounted for by human reason.

I don't believe God wants me (or any of His children) to live in a way that makes sense from the world's perspective, a way I know I can "manage." I believe He is calling me—and all of us—to depend on Him for living in a way that cannot be mimicked or forged. He wants us to walk in step with His Spirit rather than depend solely on the raw talent and knowledge He's given us.

But instead of living this way, we've created a whole brand of churches that do not depend on the Spirit, a whole culture of Christians who are not disciples, a new group of "followers" who do not follow. If all God asked for were faceless numbers to fill the churches, then we would all be doing all right. Most of us would feel pretty confident. But simply having a good speaker, a service that is short and engaging, a good venue, and whatever else we add to the mix does not make a "good" or "successful" church. God intended for His bride, those who claim His name, to be much more than this.

God is not interested in numbers. He cares most about the faithfulness, not the size, of His bride. He cares about whether people are lovers of Him. And while I might be able to get people in the doors of a church or auditorium if I tell enough jokes or use enough visuals, the fact remains that I cannot convince people to be obsessed with Jesus. Perhaps I can talk people into praying a prayer, but I cannot talk anyone into falling in love with Christ. I cannot make someone understand and accept the gift of grace. Only the Holy Spirit can do that. So by every measure that actually counts, I *need* the Holy Spirit. Desperately.

———————

Sometimes I leave Christian events wondering if we resemble the prophets of Baal in 1 Kings 18 more than Elijah, the prophet of God.

If you've forgotten the story, it may be good to stop here and read that chapter, or else the rest of what I write in this section will make very little sense to you. The prophets of Baal had a loud, passionate worship gathering that lasted from morning till evening. When they were done, they had a great time of fellowship (I think you can call it that). But "no one answered; no one paid attention" (18:29). After all of that, Elijah prayed. God heard his prayer, and fire came down from heaven.

My favorite part of that story comes when it is all over and the prophets of Baal are saying, "The LORD—he is God! The LORD—he is God!" (18:39 NIV). They didn't say, "Elijah is a great speaker" or "Elijah sure knows how to connect with God!" They were stunned by *God*. They were in awe of His power. They knew that what they experienced could not have been manipulated by Elijah. They experienced the power of God.

Is that what happens at the Christian gatherings you attend? Or does it feel more like what the prophets of Baal experienced before Elijah prayed? We can have a great time singing and dancing ourselves into a frenzy. But at the end of it, fire doesn't come down from heaven. People leave talking about the people who led rather than the power of God.

This principle carries into the way we live our personal lives as well. People ought to see the transformation in our lives and respond by saying, "The Lord—He is God!"

Has anyone ever been amazed by your peace? Love? Joy? Have they ever envied your self-control? Have you ever prayed that God would so fill you with the Spirit that people would know the change could be empowered only by the Spirit? It is when we are filled with true peace and hope that people notice there is something different about us. The Holy Spirit is the one who gives us both peace (Rom. 14:17) and hope (15:13).

I think we all could agree that living "according to our sinful flesh" is not what is intended for us as children of God. Yet even so, we often choose to face life's issues and circumstances in exactly the same way as someone without the Spirit of God. We worry, strive, and grieve no differently than unbelievers. While it is true that we are humans like everyone else, it is also true that we are humans with the Spirit of God dwelling in us. Yet, whether consciously or not, we essentially say to God, "I know You raised Christ from the dead; but the fact is my problems are just too much for You and I need to deal with them by myself."

Even in our daily living we can look more like the prophets of Baal as we live our lives, running about in a frenzy, trying to fix our problems, not stopping long enough to call on the power of God Almighty. Yet as children of God, we are not called to trust in our idols or ourselves. We are made to be like Elijah, who did not question whether God would show His face that day. He prayed and asked for help, and God sent down fire from heaven in response.

Perhaps you don't need fire from heaven, but peace. Perhaps what you need is wisdom to know which decision to make. Or courage to do the right thing, even though you might lose your job. Or maybe you need love because you feel alone. Or you want people with a similar vision to journey with and support you along the way. Whatever you need, the point is that God is aware of you and your circumstances, and He knows what you really need. He is able to bring these things, people, and circumstances into your life.

But God is not a coercive God. And though He desires for His children to know peace and love and to have wisdom, I have noticed that often He waits for us to ask.

He desires to do more than "help out" a bit. He wants to completely transform us. He wants to take a timid heart and set it ablaze with strength and courage, so much so that people know something supernatural has taken place—life change just as miraculous as fire coming down from heaven. He wants to imbue us with His wisdom because He is the "spirit of wisdom and revelation" (Eph. 1:17; see Isa. 11:2). Even as the Spirit works in us to make us more like Christ, to transform us, He is also patient. This work will not be complete until His kingdom comes in full, though this does not deter Him from working now.

———

You are most likely familiar with the "fruit passage" in Galatians 5, which says, "But the fruit of the Spirit is love, joy, peace, patience, kindness, goodness, faithfulness, gentleness and self-control. Against such things there is no law" (vv. 22–23 NIV). You may even have the list memorized. But look over those traits right now and ask yourself if you possess each to a supernatural degree. Do you exhibit more kindness and faithfulness than the Mormons you know? Do you have more self-control than your Muslim friends? More peace than Buddhists? More joy than atheists? If GOD truly lives in you, shouldn't you expect to be different from everyone else?

What disturbs me most is when we're not really bothered that God living *in* us has not made much of a noticeable difference. Most churchgoers are content to find a bit of peace rather than a "peace of God, which surpasses all understanding" (Phil. 4:7). We want just enough peace to survive the week (or perhaps even the day).

Certainly there have been times in my life when just getting through the day was possible only with God's supernatural help and presence. You might understand the kind of desperate season I am talking about; most of us have experienced times like this—times when we really do have to ask for peace and sustenance every ten minutes. But what I am talking about is when we live our lives this way, when every day of our lives we are just barely hanging on, looking no different from the rest of the world.

When we exhibit the peace that surpasses the world's understanding, that's when the world notices. *That's* when people say, "Your Lord—He is God!"

Now, this chapter is not meant to make you feel guilty. But it *is* meant to be a challenge and make a space for you to take an honest look at yourself. Do you know what it's like to be filled with joy? Do you experience genuine peace regardless of your life circumstances? Do you consistently respond with kindness no matter what you receive from others?

Can you imagine what it would be like never to get stressed-out or to worry because you are so filled with the peace and love of God?

Don't you want to be characterized by these attitudes? Don't we all want peace, and self-control, and all the rest?

Notice that the subject ("fruit") in this verse is singular. It does not say that there are many *fruits* of the Spirit, but that one fruit incorporates all the different elements that follow (love, joy, peace, etc.). This certainly doesn't make it any easier.

I don't know about you, but I cannot simply muster up more love. I can't manufacture patience just by gritting my teeth and determining to be more patient. We are not strong or good enough, and it doesn't work that way. None of us can "do goodness" on our own, much less all the other elements that make up the fruit of the Spirit.

But despite our inability to change ourselves in this way, to simply become more peaceful or joyful, we expend a great deal of effort trying. We focus on what God wants us to *do* and forget the kind of people He wants us *to be*.

Instead of mustering up more willpower, let's focus our energies and time on asking for help from the One who has the power to change us. Let's take the time to ask God to put the fruit of His Spirit into our lives. And let's spend time with the One we want to be more like.

I know in my own life I don't just want to do what my mentors do; I also want to spend time with them. I have found that through spending time with those I respect, I become more like them than I would by simply trying to "do what they do." Grunting and saying through clenched teeth, "I *will* be patient!" hasn't worked yet, and that isn't likely to change. But what does effect change is when we begin to ask God to make these fruit manifest in our lives, by the power of His Spirit, and when we spend time in communion with our God.

My favorite verse is quite possibly James 5:17, which reads, "Elijah was a man with a nature like ours, and he prayed fervently." Don't keep yourself from praying desperately and courageously for the Spirit to work in your life simply because you are not the prophet Elijah. As this verse says, Elijah was a human being with a nature like ours. He was just like us. The key thing about him? *He prayed fervently.*

Have you ever thought to yourself, "I'm praying to the exact same God Elijah prayed to"? Do you genuinely believe that Moses, Esther, David, and Daniel had *no* advantage over you spiritually? In fact, some would argue that you have the advantage of both the risen Christ and the indwelling Spirit. Let's stop looking at the godly men and women in Scripture as though their prayer lives are unattainable! Pray fervently, knowing that Peter and Paul and Mary and Ruth were men and women "with a nature like ours" (James 5:17). I know that I tend to run from situations where I *need* God, and I think that is true of almost every one of us. It is safer to avoid situations where we need God to come through than to stake it all on Him and risk God's silence. If Elijah had not had the courage to face down the prophets of Baal that day, if he hadn't prayed fervently and courageously, then he would not have experienced God's power in such a profound way. But in moments of doubt, I can't help but think, *What if God hadn't sent down fire that day and Elijah ended up in the same predicament as the prophets of Baal? What then?*

This is certainly not a call to demand that God prove Himself in each and every circumstance that we manufacture. But it is a profound reminder that God delights in showing up when His people are in desperate need of Him, because that means no one else can steal His glory.

───────

Let's delve into the Old Testament once again and look at the story of Gideon in Judges 7. Gideon started with an army thirty-two thousand men strong. In several stages, God purposely dwindled it to three hundred men. I think God did this so that no one could say, "Look what we did!" Instead, everyone knew that it was God's power that defeated the enemy. Only through God could a tiny army of three hundred men rout the much larger Midianite army.

God wants the praise for what we do in our lives. But if we never pray audacious, courageous prayers, how can He answer them? If we never follow Him to positions where we need Him, how can He show up and make His presence known?

Can you, along with Elijah and Gideon, say that when people see your life they respond by praising our Father?

When I live by my own power and strength, relying solely on my natural talents to see me through, then people naturally praise me for how I am living. But when I am living in a way that requires me to depend on the Holy Spirit, people respond by praising my Father in heaven.

───────

When was the last time you experienced the hand of God? Ask yourself. Think about the times in your life when you have been touched by God in a way that no one could convince you was a coincidence. These may not be "fire from heaven" or "voice like thunder" kinds of experiences; perhaps it was the wordless whisper of hope when you were overwhelmed by depression. Or perhaps you experienced God through the unconditional acceptance of another human being. Or maybe you glimpsed some of His character through a sunset that just made you stop and worship. We experience God through a variety of means, and God delights to communicate and share Himself with His beloved daughters and sons.

The Holy Spirit is present throughout the New Testament as well as the Old Testament. I believe in Him because I believe the Scriptures. But even if you took away what I "know" about the Holy Spirit from reading the Scriptures, my "right answers" about the Holy Spirit, I would still believe.

I would still believe in the Spirit because I have experienced God the Holy Spirit working in and through and around my life in ways I cannot deny or ignore. I certainly do not advocate ignoring the Scriptures or basing everything on experience, but to completely ignore experience—including your personal experience and the experience of the wider body of Christ, both now and historically—is unbiblical.

If you have not known and experienced God in ways you cannot deny, I would suggest that you are not living in a needy and dependent way. God delights to show up when His children call on His name and when they are trusting fully in Him to come through, whether that is in relationships, in battling sin, in strength to make sacrifices, or in endurance to be faithful in daily life. Are you living this way? Or are you surviving only by your own strength, by your own wits?

We Were Family

A while back a former gang member came to our church. He was heavily tattooed and rough around the edges, but he was curious to see what church was like. He had a relationship with Jesus and seemed to get fairly involved with the church.

After a few months, I found out the guy was no longer coming to the church. When asked why he didn't come anymore, he gave the following explanation: "I had the wrong idea of what church was going to be like. When I joined the church, I thought it was going to be like joining a gang. You see, in the gangs we weren't just nice to each other once a week—we were family." That killed me because I knew that what he expected is what the church is intended to be. It saddened me to think that a gang could paint a better picture of commitment, loyalty, and family than the local church body.

The church is intended to be a beautiful place of community. A place where wealth is shared and when one suffers, everyone suffers. A place where when one rejoices, everyone rejoices. A place where everyone experiences real love and acceptance in the midst of great honesty about our brokenness. Yet most of the time this is not even close to how we would describe our churches.

Without the Spirit of God in our midst, working in us, guiding us, and living and loving through us, we will never be the kind of people who make up this kind of community. There is no such thing as a real believer who doesn't have the Holy Spirit, or a real church without the Spirit. It's just not possible. But what is possible is that we would individually and corporately quench and hinder the Spirit's activity in and through our lives.

As for me, I am tired of talking about what we are going to do. I am sick of talking about helping people, of brainstorming and conferencing about ways we can be radical and make sacrifices. I don't want to merely talk anymore. Life is too short. I don't want to speak about Jesus; I want to know Jesus. I want to be Jesus to people. I don't want just to write about the Holy Spirit; I want to experience His presence in my life in a profound way.

A few months ago, the elders at Cornerstone Church began to ask the question "Why don't we live like the believers who made up the first church?" In Acts 2:42–47 we read the following:

> They devoted themselves to the apostles' teaching and to fellowship, to the breaking of bread and to prayer. Everyone was filled with awe at the many wonders and signs performed by the apostles. All the believers were together and had everything in common. They sold property and possessions to give to anyone who had need. Every day they continued to meet together in the temple courts. They broke bread in their homes and ate together with glad and sincere hearts, praising God and

enjoying the favor of all the people. And the Lord
added to their number daily those who were being
saved. (TNIV)

What followed was a beautiful time of sharing as our elders laid
"everything" at one another's feet. We surrendered the keys to our
cars, homes, and bank accounts. The elders looked me in the eyes
and said, "What's mine is yours. If anything ever happens to you, I
will support and care for your kids *as much as* I would care for my
own. I will be your life insurance." And because they had a history
of genuine sacrifice for the sake of the gospel, I believed what they
said.

From there, we began going to some of our friends in the
congregation and expressing our commitment to them. And now
this mentality is spreading. New life is permeating the church as
individuals back up their words with sacrifice. Cars and homes are
being sold or given away. Expensive vacations are joyfully replaced
with caring for others. People are being welcomed into others'
homes—not only for meals, but to live. This is a small example of
the kinds of things that happen when people start to walk with the
Spirit and ask the Holy Spirit to affect every part of their lives.

I just shared about what a few people in one church in one
city in one country are doing. What else might it look like when
people begin to walk with the Spirit, submitting everything to
Him? Dream a little with me. This will look different in various
cultures around the world. The Spirit will lead believers in Beijing
to do different things from believers in the United Kingdom or
Argentina.

This is just a hint of what happens when we begin to actually live like we need the Spirit. For us at Cornerstone Church, it is only the beginning.

Forceful or Forced?

When I read the book of Acts, I see the church as an unstoppable force. Nothing could thwart what God was doing, just as Jesus foretold: "The gates of hell shall not prevail against it" (Matt. 16:18). The church was powerful and spreading like wildfire, not because of clever planning, but by a movement of the Spirit. Riots, torture, poverty, or any other type of persecution couldn't stop it. Isn't that the type of church movement we all long to be a part of?

So much of what we see today is anything but unstoppable. It can easily be derailed by the resignation of a pastor or an internal church disagreement or budget cuts. Churches we build only by our own efforts and not in the strength of the Spirit will quickly collapse when we don't push and prod them along. I spent years asking God to be part of whatever I was doing. When I read the book of Acts, I see people privileged to play a part in what God was doing.

Recently we held a discussion about how to solve some of the evident problems in our church. One of our pastors spoke up and said, "I think we're trying too hard." He went on to share of the supernatural things that had taken place through his prayer life. At that point, we decided to stop talking and thinking. The next hour was spent intensely in prayer. We never got "back to business" that day. While there is a time to brainstorm and think and act well using the gifts God has given us, far too often we never get to prayer (much less start, end, and allow it to permeate all that we do). Let's pray that God would build His church, an unstoppable force, empowered and sustained by the Holy Spirit.

―――――――――

No matter where you live and what your days look like, you have the choice each day to depend on yourself, to live safely, and to try to control your life. Or you can live as you were created to live—as a temple of the Holy Spirit of God, as a person dependent on Him, desperate for God the Spirit to show up and make a difference. When you begin living a life characterized by walking with the Spirit, that is when people will begin to look not to you but to our Father in heaven and give Him the praise.

My prayer as I've written this book is that it would not merely add to your knowledge. Maybe that sounds strange, but I mean it. Often in Christian circles we talk about truth in lieu of applying it to our lives. We hear an incisive sermon, discuss at lunch afterward how "great" or "powerful" it was, and then never think about it again, much less allow the Spirit to change us through it. The truth is that greater knowledge does not necessarily equal greater spirituality. Knowledge can lead to greater intimacy and a deeper relationship with God, but this is not an automatic effect.

Our Scriptures teach that if you know what you are supposed to do and you don't do it, then you sin (James 4:17). In other words, when we stock up on knowledge without applying it to our lives, we are actually sinning. You would think that learning more *about* God would be a good thing ... and it can be. But when we gain knowledge *about* God without responding *to* Him or assimilating His truth into our lives, then it is not a good thing. According to the Bible, it's sin.

May we not merely gain knowledge. Instead, as we learn, may we grow and confess and change more into the people we've been created to be by the power of the Holy Spirit, who dwells within us. "For the kingdom of God is not a matter of eating and drinking but of righteousness and peace and joy in the Holy Spirit" (Rom. 14:17).

The Final Biography

What if this last biography were about your life? What would be written here? Would we read stories about the indwelling work of the Holy Spirit or stories about what you have accomplished on your own? Don't be discouraged if there is not a lot of the Holy Spirit's working in your past. Pray in complete faith right now. Ask God to have His Spirit work so mightily in you that it would make for an amazing biography. A biography that speaks of a life so supernatural that no one would even consider giving you the glory. A biography that displays the power of the Spirit and lifts up the name of Jesus to the glory of God the Father. Amen.

AFTERWORD

My hope and prayer for you, the reader, is that church people don't try to normalize you. What I mean is that we often try to calm people down who are just too passionate or too sacrificial and radical. I know at times I have done this to other people. And I've had it done to me.

Two years ago at a dinner I sat next to a man who runs a human-trafficking awareness organization. He described how these children, most of whom were sold or abducted into the sex trade, are raped and abused every single night, again and again, how they have no one to advocate for them, and how there is no way out.

That night I lay awake in my bed for hours—literally hours—and I imagined my own children in this situation. Maybe that was a stupid thing to do, but suddenly, vividly, I was sobbing and I couldn't get the images out of my mind. I started thinking about what I would do if this really happened to my little girl. I know that I wouldn't stop until I had saved her. I would mobilize everyone I know through whatever means possible to get them to help. Lying there in my bed that night I got more and more passionate about everything I would do to save my little girl.

Then something happened. I am not one of those people who often hears God's distinct, clear voice (though I know some people do), but on this night, the Spirit of God said to me: *I want you to love them as your own children.* This was overwhelming to me. After all, if I treated these kids as though they were my own, I wouldn't stop praying for them. I also wouldn't stop passionately begging people to figure out ways to seek them out and rescue them. I literally wept for hours. The thought of these precious children of mine being taken advantage of was unbearable. I was now on a mission. A mission from God.

I remember getting back to Cornerstone and "rallying the troops." I was so fired up, and I got others fired up. But over the course of several months I got distracted. People around me started calming me down about sex trafficking. They said, "Francis, you can't save the world," and "You're already doing so much. Don't be so hard on yourself." And the passion I believe God gave me for children in the sex-slave trade slowly eked out of me.

Things like this happen all the time. As a church, we tend to do this to people who are passionate and bold. We mellow them out. Institutionalize them. Deaden them to the work that the Spirit is doing in them. In Acts 4:13 we read of the early church doing just the opposite. Peter and John testified before the Sanhedrin and "when they saw the courage of Peter and John and realized that they were unschooled, ordinary men, they were astonished and they took note that these men had been with Jesus" (NIV). The people were astonished at their courage and that they were uneducated. Right after Peter and John were released, they returned to the other believers and prayed for even more boldness and courage (4:29). Some of the boldest people (John and Peter) were the ones asking for more boldness!

Why don't we do this today? I have found that we generally do the opposite. Instead of encouraging people who are doing courageous things for God and joining them in their discernment process of how to be faithful to what God is calling them to, we tell them to slow down and back off. Instead of being astonished at believers' courage, frequently (and unfortunately) I am astonished at believers' timidity and lack of boldness. What a contrast to the biblical model we are given!

A few months ago I was speaking at a summer camp, and I was speaking to one of the organizations there that sponsors children. This volunteer told me about a sixteen-year-old girl there at the camp who sponsors fourteen children, on her own. I was astonished by this. Fourteen children (at about thirty dollars a month for each child) is a lot of money for a high school student to come up with. I talked to this girl and asked her how she did it. She told me that she works year-round and she works three jobs in the summertime to pay for the child support. While other teenagers are saving for a car, she's saving lives! Instead of spending her hard-earned money on herself and her future, she gives it to these fourteen children because she believes God loves them just as much as He loves her.

My prayer is that churchgoers will not dissuade her from this calling. That they won't tell her things like, "You really need to start thinking about yourself now. Your future and your education are important. What you've done is great, but it's time to think about what's next for you." Maybe this girl will stand strong in her conviction that the children she is supporting around the world are as important as she is … just maybe she won't be convinced out of her passionate love and sacrifice.

My wife and I recently decided to give all of the royalties from my previous book, *Crazy Love,* to the Isaiah 58 Fund. All of the money goes to the needy in the world—the starving, sick, impoverished, and to those in the sex-slave trade. We reasoned that if we kept all this money, we would end up spending it on things we didn't need. We knew that in the long run (eighty years from now), there would be no regrets. But if we bought things that wouldn't last beyond our time on earth, we would end up disappointed and regretful. I was a bit shocked and discouraged by some of the responses we received.

People told us that we were being foolish and irresponsible with the gifts God gave us. They said we should have at least put some away in case of an emergency. My response back was, "Is it not an emergency that children in Cambodia and Thailand and even the United States are being raped every single day of their lives? Why is that not an emergency?" I think the church often inadvertently teaches that the sex-slave trade is not an emergency. And this, I believe, is sin. Is an emergency only an emergency if it affects me and my immediate family?

I am not saying that every person is supposed to give all the money from their jobs to support children. Or that everyone has to create a fund from the royalties of their books. Or that each and every person is meant to get involved with organizations that work against the sex-slave trade. What I am saying, though, is that instead of thinking and telling people they are crazy when they feel like the Spirit is leading them into something that doesn't necessarily make sense to us, we should join them in the discernment process. Instead of discouraging people, we should pray for more insight and boldness. Instead of deadening people to the Spirit's leading with our words and our actions, we should celebrate and join the Spirit's movement in and through them!

This is not about one specific way of living radically. It is about discerning and obeying the Spirit's voice, especially when He asks you to do something that is hard, a little beyond "normal," and that requires sacrifice. This is a twofold thing: It is both about encouraging others to obey the Spirit's leadings and about listening to and obeying His leading in your own life. Do you feel bold and powerful? Whether your answer is yes or no, all of us need to ask for more courage and boldness.

So, finally, I just want to spend these last few paragraphs praying with you, the reader.

> *Spirit, we know that we have done wrong by You. Please forgive us for grieving, resisting, and quenching You. We have resisted You through sin, through our rebellion, and through our hardness of heart. At times, we have been spiritually blind. At other times, we knew what You wanted us to do, but we chose to ignore Your promptings. Yet this is not how we want to live now.*

We need You to change us. Only through You can we truly worship. Spirit of the Lord, You are the one who brings us to a place where we can worship. You are the Spirit of truth, the Spirit of holiness, the Spirit of life. Thank You for the truth, the holiness, and the life You give us.

We need Your wisdom and understanding as we seek to live this life. Keep us from disbelief, from fear. We need Your strength to help us do what you are asking us to do and to live how You are asking us to live. Speak loudly and drown out the other voices calling us to conform to the patterns of this world.

You are the Spirit of self-control and love. Give us the self-control needed to deny our flesh and follow You. Give us a love strong enough to motivate courageous action. Manifest Yourself through us that we may serve and love Your bride, the church, as You do.

Come, Holy Spirit, come. We don't know exactly what that means and looks like for each of us yet, in the particular places You've called us to inhabit. But, nonetheless, whatever it means, we ask for Your presence. Come, Holy Spirit, come.

NOTES

1. See www.JoniandFriends.org.

2. See www.Rationalpi.com/theshelter/ and www.Labri.org.

3. Esther Ahn Kim, *If I Perish* (Chicago: Moody Publishing, 2001).

4. See www.chfus.org.

ABOUT THE COAUTHOR

Danae Yankoski graduated from Westmont College, where she studied English Literature and met her best friend, now husband, Mike. An avid reader and writer from a young age, Danae has authored, coauthored, and contributed to several books including *Things I've Learned Lately*, *Crazy Love*, and *Zealous Love: A Guide to Social Justice*. Some of Danae's favorite aspects of life include mugs of tea and thought-provoking conversation; hiking, running, growing things, and being outside; interacting with different kinds of people; and playing with her black Lab, Elliott. She and Mike recently moved to Vancouver, BC, where they are pursuing their Masters of Christian Studies.

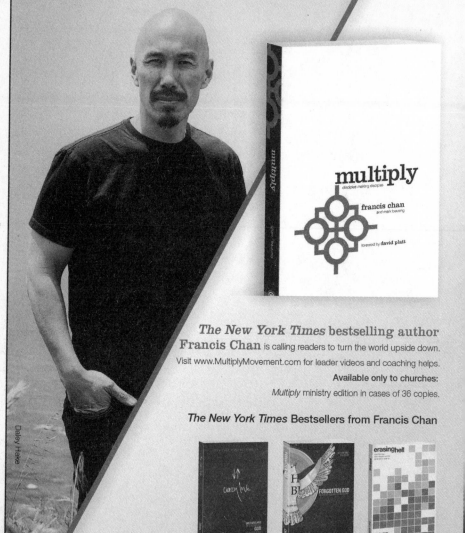